Look for these other titles in the Achieving Kicking Excellence™ series.

AXE KICK

Achieving Kicking Excellence™

Shawn Kovacich

AUTHOR APPROVED FIRST EDITION

All Rights Reserved © 2007 CHIKARA KAN—SHAWN KOVACICH

Printed in the United States of America

Library of Congress Card Number: 2004090160

ISBN #0-9707496-2-7

Table of Contents

Chapter Twelve: Preview Volume 4

Disclaimer

Please note that the author and/or publisher of this instructional book are **Not Responsible** in any manner whatsoever, for any injury, which may occur by reading and/or following the instructions located within this book. The techniques described within this book are sophisticated in nature and have the potential to cause serious damage to the reader or readers, if performed incorrectly. Therefore, it is essential that the reader or readers of this book consult a qualified and competent physician before following any of the activities, physical or otherwise, which are described within this book. This book is intended to be used as a supplemental training aid, and should be used as such, under the guidance of a qualified and competent martial arts instructor. **This book and the information contained within are intended for educational purposes only!**

Copyrights & Trademarks

Please note that no part of this book including text, photographs, and illustrations may be reproduced or transmitted in any form or by any means, graphic, electronic, or mechanical, including photocopying, recording, taping, or by any information storage retrieval system, without the express written consent of the author.

Chikara Kan, the **Chikara Kan** "**symbol**" (which is shown on the title page and the back cover), and **Achieving Kicking Excellence** are all trademarks of Chikara Kan, Inc.

Acknowledgements

I would like to take this opportunity to dedicate this book in remembrance of my closest friend and companion for many years.

Logan
November 1986 - February 13th, 2001

This book would never have been published without the assistance of the following people who have contributed their time, energy and skill in the creation of this book.

Doug and Cassie Bender for the use of their facility used in principle photography.

The staff and owners of Sports West Gym for the use of their facility and equipment used in principle photography.

Jessica Bronder for her assistance, and Ron Dunlap for his participation in this book.

"Before I studied the art, a punch to me was just a punch, a kick was just a kick. After I studied the art, a punch was no longer a punch, a kick was no longer a kick. Now that I understand the art, a punch is just a punch, a kick is just a kick." —Bruce Lee

About the Author

Watching Shawn Kovacich teach is like watching a college professor explaining quantum physics in such a way, that it is as easily understandable as a current episode of Sesame Street. With his unique ability to analyze and break down any kick to its most basic level, he then explains in exacting detail, the important aspects of each and every component in the kick. This gives the student a complete and detailed analysis of every movement in the kick from beginning to end.

Mr. Kovacich started his martial arts training at the age of seventeen, and took to it like the proverbial duck to water, earning his first-degree black belt after two years and nine months of training. His teaching ability became evident early on in his training and he often assisted his instructors with newer students.

The most influential moment of Mr. Kovacich's early martial arts training came when he was privileged to not only witness, but also to participate in two of his instructors, Shihan Brian Knechtges and Sensei Ben Hunn's, third degree black belt test, in which Shihan Knechtges and Sensei Hunn had to fight continuously for 100 minutes each against a fresh opponent every minute. Punches and kicks were not pulled and the two men were pushed beyond all normal standards of human endurance. Both men not only prevailed and were awarded their third degree black belts, but they also became a source of inspiration for Mr. Kovacich. Years later, he would take this test not once, but twice, and emerged triumphant both times.

Shortly after testing for and receiving his first-degree black belt, Mr. Kovacich accomplished another prestigious goal while participating in a charity fund-raiser. That goal, which he easily reached, was the first of what was to become two world records for endurance high kicking certified by The Guinness Book of World Records.

Mr. Kovacich has been an active instructor, teaching in as many as three schools at a time since 1985. He has taught students of all ages from six to sixty-eight, and from all walks of life, including law enforcement personnel, military personnel, correctional officers, mental health professionals, etc. Since the early 90's, he has also been an active competitor in bare knuckle full-contact karate. Competing in such prestigious tournaments throughout the United States such as the Sabaki Challenge, the Great Northwest Sabaki Satellite, the U.S. Shidokan Open, and the Shidokan Team USA. Mr. Kovacich still actively competes in these tournaments as well as being one of the top Instructor/Coaches for the former USTU (United States Tae Kwon Do Union) national and international tae kwon do competitions.

Mr. Kovacich is currently a fourth-degree black belt in both Karate and Tae Kwon Do. Powerful and intelligent, he is constantly analyzing every movement in a kick in order to get the most speed and power available. He is one of only a handful of instructors who can improve anyone's kicking ability regardless of their physical ability or non-ability, or their martial arts style. Unyielding power is what makes Shawn Kovacich a world-class fighter, but what makes him truly unique is his analytical and innovative teaching ability.

Preface

In an unarmed self-defense encounter, your kicking skills or lack thereof, can be the deciding factor between victory and defeat. I can still remember back in my high school days when kicking was considered dirty fighting, and seldom if ever used. Things certainly have changed since the late 70's and early 80's. Today kicking is not only used more frequently, but it also ranks as perhaps the most versatile and underrated weapon that you have in your personal arsenal. With the noted exception of your head, and I don't mean as a physical weapon, but in your ability to intelligently avoid the threat, and if you are unable to avoid it, to overcome it as quickly and efficiently as possible.

Presented here are several different reasons why you should learn and practice the kicking skills presented not only in this book, but also from a certified and competent martial arts instructor.

1. The majority of people do not know how to kick, and therefore tend to rely mainly on their hands, giving them only two weapons. By learning how to kick, you have doubled your available weapons from two (your hands) to four (your hands and feet).
2. Your legs are the most powerful physical weapons that you have in your arsenal. They are several times stronger than your arms and have a greater reach.
3. Kicking can be your "Ace in the Hole" when fighting. Used properly, your opponent will not expect it and will never know what hit him.
4. Kicking adds another dimension to your fighting abilities by allowing you to kick at the same time your hands are defending, attacking or grabbing your opponent.
5. If you wind up on the ground, kicking can give you that extra split second in order to keep your opponent at bay while you regain your standing position.
6. Kicking helps keep you in shape by constantly strengthening and stretching the legs and lower torso. It is all too easy to forget that your legs are carrying you around everyday. Without them where would you be?

The exact reason why you have decided to begin utilizing the kicking skills taught in this book depends upon your own personal needs and interests. You may enjoy it because of the stress reduction and physical fitness benefits, or simply because you enjoy the physical challenge that kicking correctly presents. While others enjoy the sporting, or competition aspects of the tournament arena. However for most people, their primary reason for practicing these kicking skills is for self-defense.

Irregardless of the reason, the materials presented in this book are beneficial to anyone who wants to improve their kicking ability, whether it is the martial artist, tournament competitor, aerobic kick-boxing enthusiast, or the self-defense advocate.

While this book and the material presented within it are invaluable to the individual who does not have the opportunity to learn in a formal setting, it is also a tremendous benefit to those who are fortunate enough to have access to a qualified and competent instructor. A privilege and an honor one should never take for granted.

It is my hope that every person who picks up this book and studies it, walks away with an in-depth understanding of how to correctly perform all of the intricate aspects of the Out-to-In Axe Kick and its 5 most common variations. As well as, the In-to-Out Axe Kick and its 5 most common variations. As the individual becomes increasingly proficient at performing their kicking and fighting skills, their need to exercise self-discipline, self-control, and responsibility increases dramatically.

What exactly is an Axe Kick?

I am often asked this question and the best response that I have come up with is simply this, "A properly executed Axe Kick performed by a man (or woman), can be likened to the perfectly executed swing of a lumberjack chopping a block of wood with an axe."

Note:

All of the kicks shown in this book were executed with the right leg. Therefore, in order to execute these kicks with the left leg, simply switch each kicks description from left to right and vice versa where appropriate. I have included a complete description of Back Spin Axe Kick utilizing the left leg at the end of the Out-to-In Axe Kick Variations chapter, and Switch Axe Kick utilizing the left leg at the end of the In-to-Out Axe Kick Variations chapter. Use these examples as guidelines for switching the descriptions of the other kicks when kicking with the left leg.

How To Use This Book

Although you can learn all of the techniques shown in this book on your own, there are many different subtleties and variables present within each of the kicks shown that true mastery of any of these kicks can only be gained under the knowledgeable eye of a qualified and competent instructor. This book is designed to be a reference manual for the instructor, and a textbook for the student. In order to learn from this book, you must first grasp a basic understanding on how to learn. In explaining this, I like to use the story of learning how to walk.

Every one of us, you included, came into this world as a baby. Did you run marathons as a baby? Of course not. You weren't even able to do anything for yourself, except for maybe making messes. And everybody has been through that, no matter whom or what they are, we all started out as babies. Now how does a baby first get around? Does he walk or run? No, of course not, a baby first gets around by being carried. Then as the baby's muscles get stronger and he gets a little older he starts to crawl. And in no time at all, he gets pretty good at it and watch out. He is all over the place in no time at all and seemingly faster than greased lightning. After awhile crawling gets kind of old and he begins to start learning how to walk. Mom and Dad are their holding his hand as he staggers across the room like a drunken sailor on a Saturday night.

Of course there are the falls and spills that happen as he tries walking on his own, but such is the process of learning. After a while he starts walking on his own and then comes the baby run, which if you are a parent or have ever baby sat a small child you know exactly what I am talking about. It begins with you looking away for just a second and then bang, he's off like a thoroughbred at the Kentucky Derby going for the Triple Crown, and almost as fast. Eventually the baby grows into a child and learns how to run and jump and do all kinds of things.

Of course none of these would have been possible if he hadn't first been carried, then taught to crawl, and had his hand held as he learned to walk, and perhaps just as important, received all those bumps and bruises from falling down and getting back up and trying it again.

The key to learning from this book is to be patient, start slow and take it in steps. Don't skip steps or rush the learning process. Years went into the making of this book in order to give you the best possible source of information on how to correctly execute the kicks presented within.

Go to the Doctor:
You should always consult with a qualified and competent physician before trying any of the techniques described in this book.

Read:
Take this book and read it cover to cover several times, before attempting to execute any of the techniques presented in this book.

Study and Learn:
Learn the who, what, where, when, why and how's of the anatomy and principles behind the kicks presented in this book. Remember that ignorance may be

xiv

bliss, but knowledge truly is power.

Warm-up and Stretching:

Always warm-up and stretch thoroughly and properly before participating in any physical activity. An ounce of prevention is worth a pound of cure.

Take One Step at a Time:

When writing this book, I designed it so that each kick was broken down into several different sections with several technical points in each section. All of that was done so that you could full understand how to correctly execute each of the 12 kicks presented. With the understanding that once you had learned all of the technical points in each section, that you would then put them all together until you were able to perform each movement in every section of the kick as one continuous movement.

Let's use the co-primary kick Out-to-In Axe Kick as an example, now the best way to understand this is to look at it on a mathematical level. By this I mean that you are going to learn this kick on a $1 + 1 = 2$ level. Each number one is representative of a technical point that is included in each section. For example Fighting Position has seven technical points. Here is what I mean.

1. Position of your feet = 1
2. Position of your knees = 1
3. Position of your upper body = 1
4. Position of your hands and elbows = 1
5. Position of your back = 1
6. Position of your head = 1
7. Position of your eyes = 1

For a total of 7 technical points.

Now when you look at all of the technical points in each section of an Out-to-In Axe Kick, it would look like this.

Fighting Position = $1 + 1 + 1 + 1 + 1 + 1 + 1 = 7$

Begin Arc = $1 + 1 + 1 + 1 + 1 + 1 + 1 + 1 = 8$

3/4 to Peak of Arc = $1 + 1 + 1 + 1 + 1 + 1 + 1 + 1 = 8$

Peak of Arc = $1 + 1 + 1 + 1 + 1 + 1 + 1 + 1 = 8$

Impact = $1 + 1 + 1 + 1 + 1 + 1 + 1 + 1 = 8$

Follow Through = $1 + 1 + 1 + 1 + 1 + 1 + 1 + 1 = 8$

Return to Fighting Position = $1 + 1 + 1 + 1 + 1 + 1 + 1 = 7$

For a total of 54 technical points.

What this book was designed to do was to have you fully practice each section until each of the technical points in each section becomes second nature to you. Then you will go onto the next section and do the same thing until you have learned each of the technical points in each section. After that has been accomplished, you will then put each of the sections together one at a time until you are able to perform the entire sequence of movements correctly. For example:

1. Fighting Position
2. Fighting Position + Begin Arc
3. Fighting Position + Begin Arc + 3/4 to Peak of Arc

4. Fighting Position + Begin Arc + 3/4 to Peak of Arc + Peak of Arc
5. Fighting Position + Begin Arc + 3/4 to Peak of Arc + Peak of Arc + Impact
6. Fighting Position + Begin Arc + 3/4 to Peak of Arc + Peak of Arc + Impact + Follow Through
7. Fighting Position + Begin Arc + 3/4 to Peak of Arc + Peak of Arc + Impact + Follow Through + Return to Fighting Position

Ideally you should execute any kick without conscious thought and in one single fluid motion. The execution of the kick should be instinctive in nature rather than an action or reaction, which in both cases are infinitely slower than acting instinctively. However just like a baby, you must first go through the entire learning process until executing the kick becomes as natural and without thought as breathing.

Learn the Co-Primary Kicks First:

This is pretty much self-explanatory, since everything else is based on the Out-to-In Axe Kick and the In-to-Out Axe Kick. Once you learn these co-primary kicks, all of the other variations will be much easier to learn and execute.

Practice, Practice, Practice:

I have heard it said that one must practice any given technique 1,000 times before they know it. I totally and completely disagree. You should correctly practice any technique 3,000 to 5,000 times to learn it, 10,000 times correctly to know it, and a lifetime of practice to master it.

Read this book regularly:

Use this book as a reference guide on a regular basis. As a general rule of thumb, every time you practice an Axe Kick 1,000 times you should have read this book at least once.

Quality Supervision:

Whenever possible, you should always practice under the watchful eye of a qualified and competent martial arts instructor.

Basic Anatomy of the Axe Kick

In this chapter, I will attempt to give you a basic understanding of the primary muscular groups and bones in the skeletal system that form the anatomical basis of an Axe Kick. I will do this by listing each of the muscle and bones separately and then at the end of each description, I will provide an explanation as to their role in the correct execution of an Axe Kick. Although the entire body is utilized in the correct execution of an Axe Kick, I will only be concentrating on the muscle and skeletal structure of the lower back, hips, legs and feet.

BONES:

The skeleton of the leg is composed of the femur (thigh bone), tibia and fibula (calf bones), and the patella (kneecap). These bones have three primary sites of articulation; the hip joint, formed by the head of the femur and the acetabulum of the pelvis, the knee joint, formed by the joining of the lower end of the femur, the patella, and the superior end of the tibia and fibula, and the ankle, formed by the articulation between the tibia and the tarsus. The legs are responsible for bearing a great deal of weight and are subjected to intense vertical and lateral stresses, especially at the knee joint. Consequently, the bones of the leg are often cracked or broken, and the knee, hip and ankle joint are particularly susceptible to fracture, strain, sprain, and disloca-tion.

Each foot is made up of twenty-six bones, which form the ankle, top and bottom of the foot, and toes. These bones are articularly specialized, allowing a wide range of flexibility, while being able to withstand the incredible amounts of stress placed upon them. It is estimated that each stride of an adult places 900 pounds of pressure per square inch on the bottom of the foot. Seven of these bones form the compact arrangement of the ankle, or tarsus, and the heel.

Calcaneus:

The calcaneus bone forms the lower, outer part of the ankle and extends down-ward to form the heel. It is responsible for bearing much of the immediate stress placed upon the foot during walking and running. **The back of the calcaneus or heel, is the striking implement used when executing an Axe Kick.**

Femur:

The femur is the longest bone in the body, and composes the upper leg, or thigh. The upper portion of the femur articulates with the acetabulum, the large circular cavity on each side of the pelvis, to form the ball and socket joint at the hip. The bottom portion of the femur articulates with the tibia and fibula, and the patella (knee cap) to form the knee joint. Each femur directly bears the weight of the entire upper body. **The femur provides support to the lower leg bones (tibia and fibula), at the junction of the knee joint, which lend direct support to the calcaneus bone. The head of the femur also connects to the pelvis.**

Fibula:

The fibula is the smaller of the two bones of the lower leg. It articulates at each end with the parallel tibia, at its upper portion with the femur to form the knee joint, and at its lower portion with the bones of the ankle, or tarsus. The fibula is so named

1

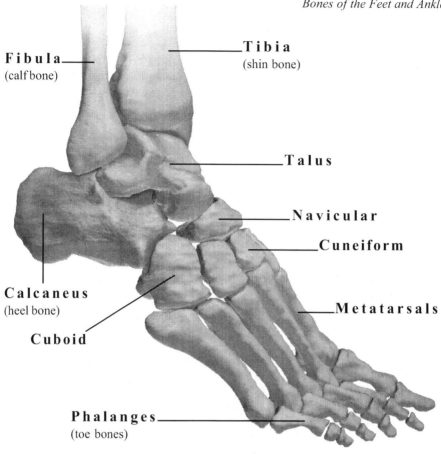

Fibula
(calf bone)

Tibia
(shin bone)

Talus

Navicular

Cuneiform

Calcaneus
(heel bone)

Metatarsals

Cuboid

Phalanges
(toe bones)

because it serves as a brace for the lower leg. **The fibula along with the tibia, lend direct support to the calcaneus bone, which is the striking implement used in an Axe Kick.**

Knee:

The knee is the hinge like joint formed by the lower end of the femur, the upper ends of the tibia and fibula, and the patella (kneecap). The knee is a joint, which is subjected to tremendous lateral stress during normal activity and is guarded by a number of ligaments to help lend it support. Even so, however, the increased stresses placed upon this joint during extreme athletic activity, which require the individual to alter directions rapidly, the knee often bears the brunt of intolerable shearing forces. Such incidences often result in torn ligaments within the knee, which require corrective surgery. Proper technique and attention to detail must be utilized at all times in order to avoid injuring yourself during the execution of any technique. **The knee due to its unique structure and function, can be easily damaged if proper technique is not used throughout the entire execution of an Axe Kick.**

2

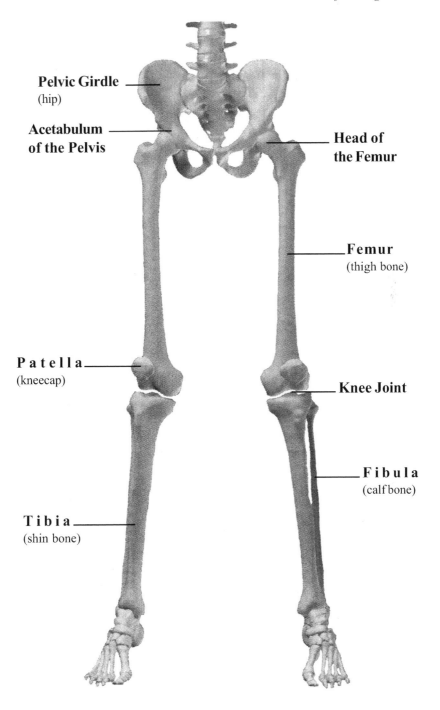

Pelvic Girdle
(hip)

**Acetabulum
of the Pelvis**

**Head of
the Femur**

Femur
(thigh bone)

P a t e l l a
(kneecap)

Knee Joint

F i b u l a
(calf bone)

T i b i a
(shin bone)

Patella:
The patella or kneecap is a small bone of the knee joint, which resembles an inverted teardrop. The patella is connected to the joint by a series of ligaments.

Pelvis:
The pelvis creates the basin of the lower abdominal cavity. It articulates with the sacrum in the back, and thereby connects to the rest of the vertebral column, and also to the legs through the ball and socket joint formed by the two acetabula of the pelvis and the head of each femur. **The pelvis is the connecting link between the actions of the upper and lower body.**

Phalanges:
The bones of the toes are known as phalanges. Each toe has three phalanges, with the exception of the large toe, which has only two. Toes and ankles are the most common self-inflicted injuries when kicking. Keeping your toes back, and out of the way, and your foot tight upon impact will greatly reduce the risk of injury. **The toes provide balance and stability in all activities that involve moving on your feet.**

Tibia:
The tibia is the primary bone of the two in the lower leg. Also called the shinbone, the tibia bears most of the weight. Its upper portion articulates with the parallel fibula, patella and the femur at the knee joint. Its lower portion articulates with the fibula and the talus of the ankle. **The tibia along with the fibula lend direct support to the calcaneus bone, which is the striking implement used in an Axe Kick.**

MUSCLES:
The muscles and joints of the legs provide strength and stability for the body. These muscles serve to transmit the weight of the body and provide power for such common activities as walking, running, and jumping. They also absorb the cumulative impact of those activities. The leg bones are girded on all sides by sets of powerful muscles that allow the legs to bend (flexion) and straighten (extension) as well as move outward from the body (abduction) and inward (adduction). Some of these muscles are relatively long and participate in more than one type of movement. The thigh consists of the body's largest bone, the femur, which is bound on all sides by sets of powerful muscles.

The calf, ankle and foot are controlled largely by a series of muscles and tendons that function as a single biomechanical unit. These muscles work together to lift or lower the heel for virtually any activity that involves locomotion. All of the parts of the lower leg are interconnected. For example, when you stand on your toes, you can feel the muscles in the back of your calf doing most of the work. Because of its structure, and because it absorbs the impact from activities like running and jumping, the lower leg is subject to more exercise related injuries than any other area of the body. These problems range from bunions and blisters to stress fractures and ankle sprains, the most common sports injury of all.

The feet and toes are essential elements in body movement. They bear and propel the weight of the body during walking and running, and help to maintain balance during changes of body position. The foot can adapt itself to different surfaces and

4

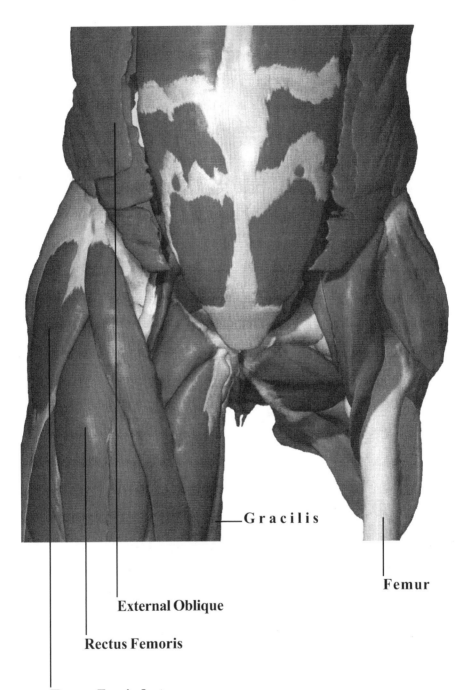

Gracilis

Femur

External Oblique

Rectus Femoris

Tensor Fascia Latae

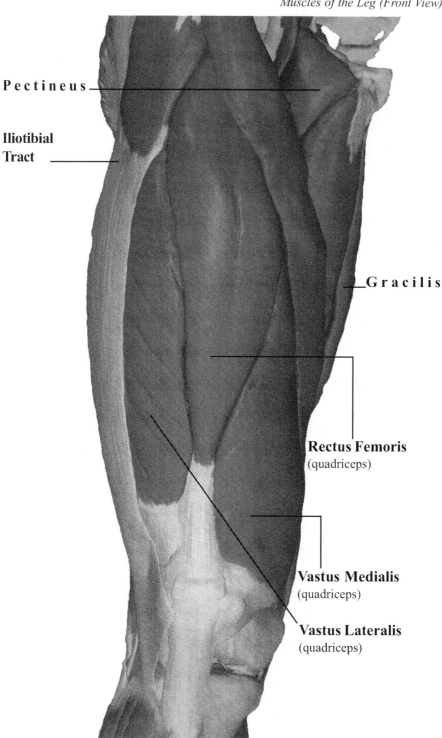

Pectineus

**Iliotibial
Tract**

Gracilis

Rectus Femoris
(quadriceps)

Vastus Medialis
(quadriceps)

Vastus Lateralis
(quadriceps)

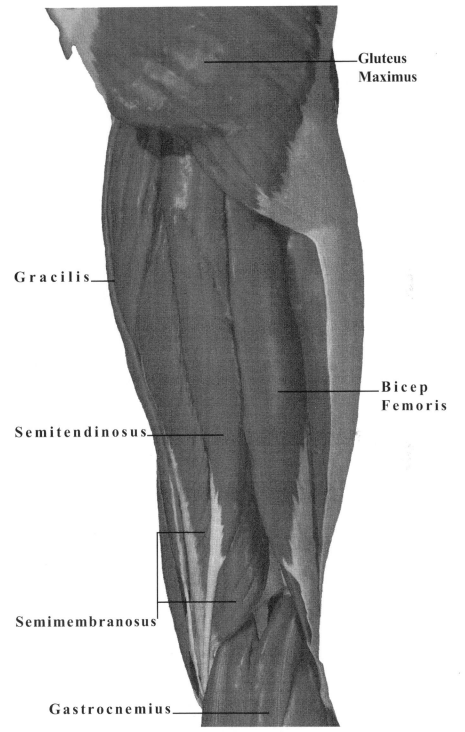

Gluteus
Maximus

Gracilis

Bicep
Femoris

Semitendinosus

Semimembranosus

Gastrocnemius

7

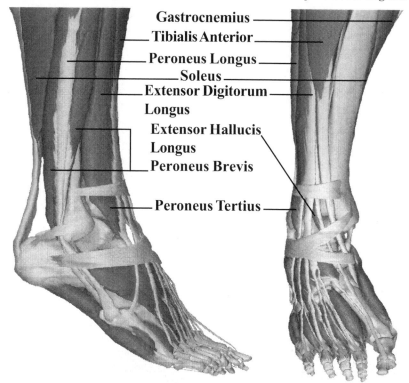

Gastrocnemius
Tibialis Anterior
Peroneus Longus
Soleus
Extensor Digitorum
Longus
Extensor Hallucis
Longus
Peroneus Brevis

Peroneus Tertius

absorb mechanical shocks as well. Each foot has about thirty-three muscles, some of which are attached to the lower leg.

Bicep Femoris:

The bicep femoris muscle runs from the tuberosity of the ischium down to the back of the head of the fibula. This muscle flexes the lower leg at the knee joint and also abducts or rotates the tibia outward. **This muscle helps extend the leg from the "Peak of Arc" position to "Impact" and continuing through to the "Follow Through" position. It also acts as a stabilizer and somewhat like a "shock absorber" for the knee itself during impact with the target.**

Extensor Digitorum Longus:

The extensor digitorum longus muscle arises from the tibia and the front of the fibula, and runs down into the foot and the toes. This muscle extends the toes and flexes the foot toward the leg. **This muscle assists in pushing off the floor with your toes during the "Begin Arc" phase of executing an Axe Kick. It also flexes the foot toward your knee in order to obtain the proper foot position for an Axe Kick.**

Extensor Hallucis Longus:

The extensor hallucis longus muscle lies deep in the lower leg and extends down to the big toe. This muscle extends the big toe and assists in flexing the foot. **As with the extensor digitorum longus, this muscle assists in pushing off the floor**

8

with your big toe during the "Begin Arc" phase of executing an Axe Kick. It also flexes the foot toward your knee in order to obtain the proper foot position for an Axe Kick.

External Oblique:
The external oblique muscle runs along the side of the torso and partially on the front from the lower ribs to the rectus, the pubis bone, and iliac crest of the hip. This muscle assists the rectus abdominus muscle in flexing the spine when the trunk twists or turns. **This muscle assists with the flexing of the spine and abdomen when executing an Axe Kick.**

Flexor Digitorum Longus:
The flexor digitorum longus muscle runs deep in the lower leg from the middle of the tibia to underneath the foot to the toes. This muscle assists to flex the toes during the final push off in walking or running. **As with the extensor digitorum longus and the extensor hallucis longus, this muscle assists in pushing off the floor with your toes during the "Begin Arc" phase of executing an Axe Kick.**

Gastrocnemius:
The gastrocnemius muscle runs from the back of the knee to the ankle to form the calf muscle. This muscle propels the body when walking, running or jumping. It raises the heel, which lifts the body. It also assists, though minimally, in flexing the knee joint. **This muscle assists the bicep femoris in rasing the heel of your foot off the ground when you begin to initiate an Axe Kick.**

Gemelli:
The gemelli are two small muscles of the hip. The muscles arise from the spine and insert into the upper edge of the thighbone. These muscles help rotate the thigh. **This muscle helps rotate the thigh when you first begin to initiate an Axe Kick by raising your leg up from the "Begin Arc" position to the "Peak of Arc" position.**

Gluteus Maximus:
We sit on the largest and most powerful muscle in our body, the gluteus maximus. This muscle powerfully extends the thigh at the hip joint and moves it away from the body, as when walking or running. **This muscle helps raise the leg up to the "Peak of Arc" position, as well as extending the leg from there to "Impact" and continuing through to the "Follow Through" position. Proper utilization of this muscle will greatly increase the power in your Axe Kick.**

Gluteus Medius:
The gluteus medius runs from the outer portion of the pelvis, up to the crest of the pelvis. The gluteus medius is partially covered by the gluteus maximus. It moves the thigh outward and rotates it, as when walking or running. It keeps the torso upright during walking when one foot is touching the ground and the other is not. **This muscle assists in raising the leg up to the "Peak of Arc" position.**

Gracilis:
The gracilis muscle lies on the inside of the femur and begins at the pubic arch and runs down towards the inside of the tibia or shinbone. This muscle brings the knee up and pulls it across the front, toward the middle of the body. It also assists in rotation of the leg. **This is the primary muscle utilized when raising the thigh up**

9

towards the abdomen from the "Begin Arc" position to the "Peak of Arc" position.

Iliopsoas:
The iliopsoas runs from deep in the back of the abdomen towards its insertion on the back of the femur. This muscle flexes the hip and assists in abduction and outward rotation of the hip. **This muscle assists in flexing the thigh towards the abdomen and assists in raising the leg up to the "Peak of Arc" position.**

Iliotibial Tract:
The iliotibial tract begins at the upper edge of the femur and ends where it inserts into the condyle of the tibia. It acts almost like a ligament, by helping mainly to stabilize the knee joint, but also acts in flexing (bending) and extending (straightening) the knee. **This muscle assists in straightening and stabilizing the knee during the execution of an Axe Kick.**

Pectineus:
The pectineus muscle lies on the front of the upper and middle part of the thigh. This muscle flexes and moves the thigh towards the body and rotates it towards the center. **This muscle helps flex the hip creating added force (not speed) to the Axe Kick. It also assists with bringing the kicking leg back down from the "Peak of Arc" position to "Impact" and continuing through to the "Follow Through" position.**

Peroneus Brevis:
The peroneus brevis muscle runs along the outside of the lower half of the fibula or lower leg. This muscle works with the peroneus longus to extend the foot. **This muscle helps extend the foot as when pushing off the floor to move into the "Begin Arc" position.**

Peroneus Longus:
The peroneus longus muscle runs along the upper part of the outside of the fibula or lower leg. This muscle works with the peroneus brevis to extend the foot. **This muscle, along with the peroneus brevis, helps extend the foot as when pushing off the floor to move into the "Begin Arc" position.**

Peroneus Tertius:
The peroneus tertius runs from the lower third of the fibula downward and slightly forward, across the ankle and inserts into the little toe. This muscle provides dorsiflexion and eversion of the foot. **This muscle helps the foot maintain its proper position in order to execute an Axe Kick.**

Plantaris:
The plantaris muscle runs from the lower end of the femur down to a small area on the bottom of the calcaneus or heel bone. This muscle works with the gastrocnemius to extend the ankle if the foot is free, and bend the knee if the foot is fixed, as when walking. **This muscle helps extend the foot as when pushing off the floor to move into the "Begin Arc" position.**

Popliteal Region:
The popliteal muscle starts from the femur and the ligament behind the knee joint and extends down to the shaft of the tibia or shinbone. This muscle assists in rotat-

ing the tibia and is used when bending the knee. **This muscle is used to slightly bend the knee on the kicking leg prior to impact.**

Quadriceps:

The quadriceps consists of four separate muscles. The rectus femoris, which runs from the ilium or hipbone down to the knee. This muscle flexes the hip joint and helps with hip joint abduction. The vastus lateralis is located halfway down the outside of the thigh, this muscle extends the knee, but it needs the vastus medialis in order to give a straight pull to the knee. The vastus intermedius lies between the vastus medialis and the vastus lateralis, and beneath the rectus femoris. This muscle extends the knee with its pull directly upward on the patella. And finally the vastus medialis, which is located above the knee, on the top of the thigh. This muscle extends the knee with the assistance of the vastus lateralis. These muscles cover the front and sides of the femur or thigh, and work together as a primary extensor of the knee. The rectus femoris muscle extends the leg at the knee joint and flexes the thigh at the hip joint. **The rectus femoris primarily flexes the thigh towards the abdomen and assists in raising the leg up to the "Peak of Arc" position. All four-quadriceps muscles work together to straighten the knee when executing an Axe Kick.**

Semimembranosus:

The semimembranosus muscle begins in the tuberosity of the ischium or underneath and back of the pelvis, and runs two-thirds of the way down the back of the thigh to the outer condyle of the femur or upper leg, just above the knee. This muscle extends the thigh and assists with the inward rotation of the hip joint. It also provides flexion and inward rotation for the knee. **This muscle along with the semitendinosus assists in extending the thigh from the "Peak of Arc" position to "Impact" and continuing through to the "Follow Through" position.**

Semitendinosus:

The semitendinosus muscle begins in the ischium or bottom and back of the pelvis, and runs two-thirds of the way down the middle of the back of the thigh. It is considered one of the hamstring muscles. This muscle flexes the lower leg and extends the thigh at the hip joint. It also provides flexion and inward rotation for the knee. **This muscle along with the semimembranosus assists in extending the thigh from the "Peak of Arc" position to "Impact" and continuing through to the "Follow Through" position.**

Soleus:

The soleus muscle is located on the back of the lower leg and runs from the upper part of the fibula down to the middle portion of the calcaneus or heel bone. This muscle is used to point the foot or raise the heel, which lifts the body. **This muscle raises the heel off the floor when you begin to initiate an Axe Kick.**

Tensor Fascia Latae:

The tensor fascia latae muscle is located on the outer front corner of the ilium or hipbone. It connects the ilium to the tissues of the outer thigh. This muscle flexes, abducts, and medially rotates the thigh. **This muscle assists in the raising of the leg up to the "Peak of Arc" position.**

11

Tibialis Anterior:
The tibialis anterior muscle sits on the front of the tibia, and originates from the outside of the tibia below the knee and runs down into the foot. This muscle controls the descent of the foot during walking after the heel strikes the ground. **This muscle assists in keeping your foot in the proper position in order to execute an Axe Kick.**

Tibialis Posterior:
The tibialis posterior muscle originates from the back of the tibia, behind the knee, and runs down into the foot. This muscle flexes the foot and, working with the tibialis anterior, turns the sole of the foot inward. It is the strongest support for the arch of the foot. **This muscle is responsible for adding "spring" to your foot when stepping or running.**

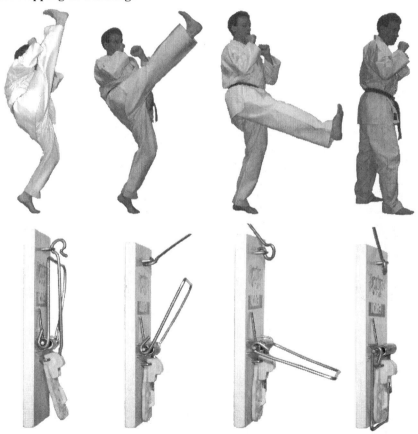

Note: Once you have reached the "Peak of Arc" position, think of your body as a mouse trap. Your base leg and body represent the wooden base, while the muscles in your leg and back represent the coiled spring. Your kicking leg is the metal striking implement, and finally the hair trigger is the slight moment of "hang time" before the trap (the Axe Kick) is sprung.

Warm Up and Stretching

Although stretching is perhaps the single greatest activity that you can perform to improve your kicking (other than utilizing proper technique), I am not going to go into great detail on the types of stretches to perform. Instead I will try and give you a firm understanding on the do's and don'ts of proper stretching. So without further delay, let's get started.

It is a well-known fact that active people tend to lead fuller more productive lives due to better health. Their endurance and stamina are greater not only during exercise, but also during normal everyday activities; such as climbing stairs, walking, doing normal household chores, etc. Medical research has shown us over the years that poor health is directly related to our increasingly sedentary life-style.

Research has also shown us that exercise, done at any age, retards the aging factor and allows our bodies to become healthier and more resistant to disease. It is obvious that as we become less active, we begin to lose not only our physical strength, but our mental strength as well. Therefore, our ability to utilize our bodies potential is greatly diminished. However, we can regain that potential and more through a correct and consistent stretching and training program.

Without a daily regiment of stretching and physical conditioning, our bodies become atrophied and weak with stored up tension, both physical and mental. Let's face it, regardless of how out of shape you are from lack of physical activity and poor eating habits, your body's potential to recover from this mistreatment and in fact flourish to new levels of health and increased physical abilities, is nothing short of phenomenal.

What does stretching do for your body? Well primarily it keeps your muscles and connective tissue flexible and more resilient to injury. It also prepares your body for more vigorous activity. Similar to starting your automobiles engine in cold weather and allowing it to idle for several minutes before driving. This idling period allows the engine of your car to warm up before the more strenuous demands of driving are placed upon it. Stretching is the idling period for your body. Stretching is essential to any martial art or combat sport, if you wish to perform at your optimum level, whether that is in the dojo, on the street, or in competition. Stretching in and of itself is easy to do, when performed correctly and consistently, and should take you between 25 to 35 minutes depending upon your level of fitness.

However, when performed incorrectly, it can actually cause injuries and impede your progress. It is for this reason that I recommend that you utilize your head when stretching and take your time. Perform the stretches correctly and slowly for the best results. Stretch at your own pace, not someone else's.

A regular program of correct stretching, will help you avoid injuries and will allow you to perform to the best of your abilities. Stretching, when performed correctly should not be painful. You should be able to feel the stretch, as it is performed in a slow, relaxing manner. Your body should not be tense nor should you force your body when stretching. Stretching should be a relaxing and warming up process, which takes place before performing a strenuous exercise.

Do Not make stretching a strenuous exercise. Your goal to achieve when stretching should be to reduce tension in the muscles, which will allow you to stretch further. Which in turn improves your level of flexibility. For the best results, stretch before and after participating in any strenuous activity, in addition to a daily stretching routine. A good stretching program can be adjusted to suit the needs of the individual. Certain characteristics to keep in mind when developing a stretching program are; type of activity involved in, personal goals, body type, current level of flexibility, and most important, your current physical condition.

Anyone who actively participates in a correct stretching program on a regular basis can become more flexible and improve their overall physical conditioning. You don't have to be able to perform the splits or be the reincarnation of Bruce Lee in order to gain flexibility, but you do have to have the desire and the willingness to train on a daily basis, and perhaps more importantly, you must learn to be patient with yourself.

Do's and Don'ts of Stretching:

Do's:
1. Wear loose fitting, yet comfortable clothing that will not impede movement and will keep your body warm in cold or inclement weather.
2. Perform a light exercise to get your body warmed up such as jumping rope, running in place, etc.
3. Hold each stretch for 10 to 30 seconds. Relax. Then go a little farther into your stretch and hold for another 10 to 30 seconds.
4. Keep your breathing slow and under control.
5. Keep track of the time during each stretch by slowly counting to yourself.
6. When your are performing the stretch correctly, you should feel a mild tension in the muscles. It should not be painful.
7. Take your time when stretching.
8. Stretch every day for 25 to 35 minutes.
9. Pay attention to your body and what it tells you.

Don'ts:
1. Bounce up and down while stretching.
2. Over stretch to where it becomes painful.
3. Hold your breath while stretching.

Perhaps the greatest example of what a daily program of stretching can do for you is brought to us from the animal kingdom. The most dangerous and skillful hunters are without a doubt the cats. From the regal "king of the beasts" on the plains of Africa, to our own domestic house cats. No other animal displays such a tremendous combination of flexibility, agility and strength as the cat. Watch them and learn. Remember that Rome wasn't built in a day, and neither shall you.

Basic Principles of Movement for the Axe Kick

In this chapter, I will give you a basic understanding of the kicking principles involved in the correct execution of an Axe Kick. Although a lot of these principles are the same for the other primary kicks and their variations, there are others that are exclusive only to the Axe Kick and its variations. Study each one of these in detail until you know them inside and out. The more you know about a kick, the better you will be able to execute it.

Striking Implement:

The striking implement utilized in executing any Axe Kick, is the back center of the heel or calcaneus bone. This bone extends down from the ankle to form the heel.

When an Axe Kick is properly executed, with the back of the heel as the striking surface, the bones and muscles of the ankle, lower leg, upper leg and hip provide additional support upon impact with the target. As you can see, especially in the side view of the foot, there is no support if you utilize any other portion of the foot, or leg (Achille's Tendon), to execute an Axe Kick.

Remember, the idea is not to inflict damage upon yourself, but rather to your opponent when executing an Axe Kick. Therefore, you must constantly be aware of your foot position and proper striking implement every time you kick, even if you are only kicking air.

One way to produce a greater amount of force is to utilize a smaller surface area when striking your intended target. Let's say for the sake of argument that you can deliver a total of 100 lbs. of force to your target, and that the surface area of your heel is equal to 2 square inches. If you strike the target correctly with your heel, you will be delivering 50 lbs. of pressure per square inch.

However, if you strike the target incorrectly with your entire foot, which has a surface area of say 20 square inches, then you would be striking your target with 5

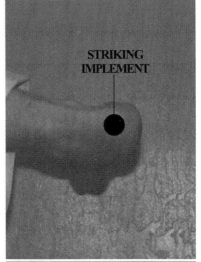

STRIKING IMPLEMENT

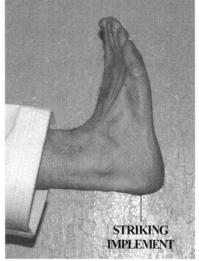

STRIKING IMPLEMENT

lbs. of pressure per square inch. Do you see what the difference is between striking with the correct surface area of the foot and the incorrect surface area? Not quite sure, let me put it to you this way. Try chopping a block of wood using the side, or even the handle of an axe to make contact with the block of wood. What happens? Now take the same block of wood and strike it correctly utilizing the sharp chopping edge of the axe. What happened this time?

Now do you see the relevancy of striking with the correct striking implement? Although the amount of force exerted against your opponent in both cases are equal, the pressure exerted upon the target struck correctly with the heel is five times greater than if you used the entire surface area of your foot. When you strike the intended target with to large a surface area, you are dissipating the force over a wider surface area resulting in a push or surface strike rather than a penetrating impact. This greatly reduces the effectiveness of your kick.

Target Areas:

I define the target area as, the general location of a vital or vulnerable point on the human body. For the greatest effectiveness with the Axe Kick in combat, you want to strike a particular vital or vulnerable point every time you strike your opponent. This will most likely deter any continued attack from your opponent by causing pain and/or injury. However, this is not always possible as very few individuals are going to stand there and let you hit them. They are going to be moving, blocking, dodging and perhaps more importantly trying to hit you back. Therefore, you want to be able to strike your opponent the most effective and efficient way that you can.

One component of that is a thorough knowledge of the vital or vulnerable points of the human body. Not only is this knowledge important to inflict damage upon your opponent (only when absolutely necessary), but also to enable you to avoid such damage being inflicted upon yourself. I am not going to discuss in detail the vital or vulnerable points in this book. However, I am going to list the general target areas and the vital or vulnerable points that lie within those areas that you will want to strike with an Axe Kick.

For more detailed information on vital or vulnerable points, please refer to the recommended reading section at the back of this book.

The effects of striking each vital or vulnerable point vary drastically depending on the accuracy, direction, speed and power utilized when striking them. Another factor that has to be taken into consideration is the human factor. Each individual is vastly different from the next and each person is going to react differently when struck. Some people may go down from the lightest of blows, while still others will merely shake off your strongest blows and keep coming at you. Which is a very good reason why you should have a thorough understanding of vital and vulnerable points.

Be prepared for any and all eventualities. Because serious injury or even death may result from forceful blows to these vital or vulnerable points, you must exercise extreme caution when practicing with a partner, and you should never actually strike any of these areas with even the lightest blows in practice. If you are called upon to strike these areas in self-defense, you should only use full force to save one's life. Along with this knowledge comes great responsibility, not only to one's self, but also to those around you. **Never Use Excessive Force!**

16

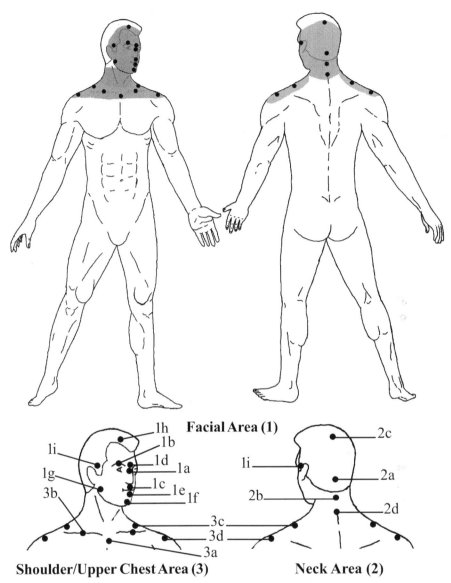

Facial Area (1)

1h
1b
1i
1d
1g
1a
3b
1c
1e
1f
1i
2c
2a
2b
2d
3c
3d
3a

Shoulder/Upper Chest Area (3)   **Neck Area (2)**

1. **Facial Area:** This target area encompasses the nose (1a), orbital bones (1b), the philtrum (1c), glabella (1d), mouth (1e), point of chin (1f), the jaw (1g), the bregma (1h), and the temple (1i).
2. **Neck Area:** This target area encompasses the occipital bone (2a), 3rd inter-vertebral space (2b), the top-back of the head (2c), and the spine (2d)..
3. **Shoulder/Upper Chest Area:** This target area encompasses the sternum (3a), collar bone (3b), brachial plexus (3c), and the shoulder joint (3d).

Each one of these vital or vulnerable points can be struck separately utilizing an Axe Kick.

17

Stability:

For the purpose of the material presented in this book, stability is defined as, "A person's ability to stand upon any given surface in a controlled and capable manner." For example you would have an easier time executing a kick on a hard flat surface such as cement or pavement, than you would if you were standing on gravel or ice. Sometimes it is necessary to create a very stable position or stance, such as when delivering a powerful kick.

Other times it is important to be in an unstable position, such as moving quickly in order to avoid being hit. Therefore a thorough understanding of the following principles will give you the ability to apply them on a daily basis, whether it be in practice, self-defense, or in competition. Several different factors contribute to one's stability such as your weight, height, center of gravity, equilibrium or balance, and your base of support. Let's take a look at each one of these factors.

Weight:

With all other factors being equal, a heavier person is generally speaking more stable than a lighter person. Consequently, a heavier person such as World Heavyweight Boxing Champion George Foreman would be harder to push off balance than a lighter person such as World Boxing Champion Oscar De LaHoya. It also stands to reason that Foreman is able to punch harder from his heavier and more solid position than De LaHoya is from his lighter and less solid position.

However, no one would argue the fact that De LaHoya, being a lighter weight fighter, has the advantage of being able to move and change direction quicker than the heavier Foreman. This is of course taking into consideration that all other factors involved are equal. I have seen some very big men that could move a lot faster and a lot smoother than their smaller counterparts.

Height and Center of Gravity:

Your center of gravity is defined as being located approximately 2 to 3 inches below your belly button and in the center of your body when standing perfectly straight with correct posture, and your feet flat on the floor. This of course varies from person to person and also upon their general body type. Women tend to have a lower center of gravity than men, and individuals with heavier legs have a lower center of gravity than someone with lighter legs. The closer one's center of gravity is to the ground or base of support, the greater their increase in stability.

You can easily change your center of gravity by bending your knees and squatting down to lower it, or by standing on your toes to raise it. You can even move your center of gravity outside your body by bending over at the waist and touching your toes. Generally speaking, the taller you are the less stability you have, while the shorter you are the more stability you have. Ask yourself this question, which has more stability the giraffe or the hippopotamus?

Equilibrium:

Equilibrium is defined as a state of balance between opposing forces. A prime example of equilibrium is a figure skaters ability to stand upon the toes of their skates while spinning their entire body into a tightly controlled blur of motion and then stopping without any outwards signs of losing their balance or equilibrium. For equilibrium to exist, your center of gravity must be centered over your base of support throughout the entire sequence of events involved when executing the Axe Kick, or any other athletic endeavor. Failure to maintain equilibrium will result in a loss of balance, and can result in a slight case of disorientation. Either of which could prove disastrous in a self-defense or tournament situation.

Base of Support:

Your base of support is described as the area of the feet upon which the weight of your body is supported, along with the space between your feet. For example,

(A) if you were standing flat footed with both feet on the ground and directly beneath your shoulders, your base of support would not only include both feet, but also the space between them.

(B) If you were standing on the toes of both feet, your base of support would include the surface area of your feet that are in direct contact with the ground and the space between them.

And

(C) if you were balancing on the ball of one foot, your base of support would be the surface area covered by the ball of your base foot.

Generally speaking, the greater the surface area of your feet that is in direct contact with the ground, and the wider the stance, the greater your base of support.

Therefore, after taking all of these factors into consideration, it stands to reason that the heavier, shorter individual is more stable during the execution of a punch when both feet are on the ground, than the lighter taller individual is when executing a kick and balancing on one leg. Does this mean that you are better off punching than kicking? Of course not, it simply means that the skills needed to kick effectively take a lot more time, effort, and attention to detail than those skills needed to punch effectively.

This is one of the reasons why so many people tend to neglect their kicking skills in favor of the easier learned punching and grappling skills. Your stance when fighting should be unstable in that you should not be set in one position, you should be constantly moving in order to avoid an attack while positioning yourself to effectively attack your opponent.

If your stance is too wide, you will sacrifice mobility as well as telegraphing any kick that you may attempt. This in effect makes you a sitting duck. If your stance is too short, you will have lost balance and stability. The ideal stance is to keep your feet shoulder width apart in length and about 4 to 8 inches apart in width.

Balance:

Although the previous section on stability also included information on equilibrium or balance, this section is devoted to balance as it applies to the execution of a kick. If you do not have good balance when kicking, not only is your kick going to be ineffective, but you may have put yourself in a dangerous situation by overextending your kicking leg, losing your balance all together, and possibly even falling to the ground. In order to prevent this, you must follow these few simple points when executing your kick.

1. Your center of gravity must be centrally located over your base foot throughout the entire kicking sequence from start to finish.

2. In order to execute your kick, it is okay to pivot on the ball of your base foot. However, the entire base foot must be in direct contact with the ground at the moment of impact, with your center of gravity in the middle of the foot, not over the ball, heel, inner or outer edge of the foot. After contact is made, you can then return the kicking foot to the starting position by once again pivoting on the ball of the base foot. You should never make contact with your target while balancing on the ball of your base foot. This incorrect technique is not only unstable, but it also causes a dramatic decrease in the effectiveness of the kick.

3. The position of your base foot is directly related to the effectiveness of maintaining your balance when kicking. For example the toes on your base foot are pointed at a 45-degree angle to your left front during the execution of an Axe Kick when kicking with the right leg, and at a 45-degree angle to your right front when kicking with the left leg. Try performing the Axe Kick with the heel of your base foot pointed at your opponent; now try it with the inside edge of your base foot pointed at your opponent. Did they work? How does your knee and hips feel?

4. And finally, don't forget the importance of that area of the body above your waist. I always find it amazing how many people forget about how important proper upper body position is to achieving and maintaining balance when kicking. Keep your head up and looking at your opponent, keep your back straight, and stop moving your arms around like a bird flapping its wings.

You'll be surprised at how much your kicks have improved by simply paying attention to these few things.

Alignment:

Your entire body should be aligned properly at the moment of impact in order to generate the maximum amount of power into the delivery of your kick upon its target. The proper body alignment at the moment of impact for the Axe Kick is as follows. Starting with the kicking foot, the heel should be the only part of the foot in contact with the target. The toes should be pointed up towards the sky and pulled back toward the kicking leg knee, which not only exposes the heel for better contact, but also tightens the ankle.

The lower leg, knee, and upper leg should all be in a straight line and supporting one another in order to increase the overall effectiveness of the kick. The kicking leg, hip, shoulder, back, and the head should all be in a straight line with the heel. The inside edge of the base leg foot is facing towards your opponent and at a 45-degree angle, while the supporting base leg is straight. This will have the effect of putting your entire body behind the kick, where the culmination of muscular speed, strength and proper technique combine to deliver the generated force into your target along a straight line of trajectory.

Sequence of Movement:

What this means is that the correct sequence of movements from the beginning stages of the kick, to the impact and subsequent follow through, should be followed in one smooth continuous motion in order to achieve the maximum effectiveness out of your kick. In order to do this however, you must first work upon each individual section of the kick until you can effectively flow from one to the other without any noticeable pauses or breaks between them. Even though the Axe Kick should be performed in one fluid motion, there are two distinct and separate sections to this kick. The first is the arcing "Path of Trajectory" of the kick from "Fighting Position" to the "Peak of Arc," and the second is the straight "Path of Trajectory," from the "Peak of Arc" to "Impact" and continuing through to the "Follow Through" and subsequent "Return to Fighting Position." Combine the two, but keep them separate.

Accuracy:

No matter how perfectly you execute your Axe Kick, it isn't going to do you one ounce of good unless you can hit your intended target. Imagine going out to war and being equipped with the biggest most powerful rifle you can get, and then not being able to hit your target. Now combine that with the fact that the guy you are fighting against is equipped with a .22 caliber rifle and the ability to hit a dime at 100 yards. Who do you think is going to survive that encounter? There are several factors involved in obtaining accurate kicks such as eye contact, proper technique, muscular control or coordination, breath control, conditioning, and most importantly, proper practice.

Eye Contact:

Your eyes should remain in constant contact with your opponent at all times. The focus of your attention should be like a flashlight on your opponent's chest, while your peripheral vision encompasses everything else from his head to his hands and down to his feet. Be careful not to focus your eyes like a laser beam on one single point, this can cause a delayed reaction time to incoming attacks and can also telegraph your intentions to your opponent.

Practice Proper Technique:

The ability to kick proficiently is not instinctive, it is a learned activity that takes years of study and constant practice to perfect. I cannot stress this simple fact enough, "Pay Attention To Detail and Practice!" The kicks presented in this book have been explained in precise detail so that you can learn the proper technique for executing them as efficiently and as accurately as possible. Practice and study the material in this book until it becomes second nature.

Muscular Control or Coordination:

This is the ability to control ones own body during physical activities such as kicking. This is not an easy skill to learn, and it takes a considerable amount of practice in order to utilize it effectively. The best method that I know of to improve your muscular control for kicking, is to perform the entire kicking sequence in slow until the point of impact, at which point you hold that position for approximately five seconds tensing your entire body during that time. After the five seconds are over, relax the entire body and slowly return to your original starting position. This should be performed at least 10 times prior to and at the end of every kicking session. Another variation of this technique is to tense all of your muscles during the entire time you are performing this exercise. This is called Dynamic Tension training and is very effective.

Breathing:
You should never hold your breath when fighting. Breathing should be done normally by inhaling through your nose and exhaling through your mouth. Remember to keep your mouth closed when fighting. Don't open it or you may get a broken jaw for your trouble. At the exact moment that you make impact with your target, you will exhale sharply, and tighten your entire body, this will add power to your kick.

Conditioning:
Physical conditioning is an absolute must if you want to perform these kicks to the best of your abilities. The better condition that you are in, the more that you will be able to do for a longer period of time before becoming fatigued. The harder you train, the easier it will become.

Strength:
Strength is the amount of muscular force that you can apply at any given time to a particular target. Don't confuse strength with power. Speed and strength are two sides of the same coin which when combined together create power. Pivoting of the hips and the turning of the body are two methods of applying strength to a kick with minimal muscular effort. I am sure you have heard of a boxer who uses only his arms when he punches rather than utilizing his entire body. The same is also true of kicking, in that the majority of individuals kick only with their legs, rather than with their entire body.

Leg strength alone does not give any real strength to the kick. Granted there is some strength present, however it is minimal compared to the strength that can be delivered if the entire body is utilized in the execution of the kick. The positioning of your head, arms, hands, and upper body are also instrumental in increasing the strength of your kick.

Speed:
The only drawbacks to kicking are that although the leg is longer than the arm, it is relatively slower, and if you don't practice your kicking skills regularly they tend to deteriorate and lose their speed. Speed and strength are two side of the same coin, which when combined together creates power. To best explain this principle I like to use the analogy of a Lamborghini and a bulldozer.

Which one of the two is faster yet not very forceful? Which one is more forceful yet slower? Obviously the Lamborghini is faster and the bulldozer is more forceful. Yet if both of these vehicles started at the same time from one mile away and they both drove as fast as they could until they hit a brick wall at the end of that mile, which one would hit first, and second? And what would happen to them? Obviously the Lamborghini traveling in excess of 200 plus miles per hour would strike the wall long before the much slower bulldozer. However, when it hit the wall it would totally destroy the car and I am sure would cause some minor damage to the wall.

The bulldozer on the other hand, would take a considerably longer amount of time to cover that distance in order to reach the wall. However, once it reached the wall, its greater strength would easily, but slowly go through it. My whole point being that your body should be like the blinding speed of the Lamborghini as your foot travels to reach its target. However, at the moment of impact, your foot and entire body should transform itself instantaneously from the blinding speed of the Lamborghini into the wall-crushing strength of the bulldozer.

Immediately after impact, your entire body should return to the blinding speed of the Lamborghini in order to facilitate a faster "Follow Through" and completion of the kick and subsequently returning to the initial starting position. A relaxed muscle is faster, while a tense or contracted muscle is slower yet stronger. Utilize this to your best advantage when executing these kicks.

Distance and Timing:

If the opponent is too far away, how are you going to hit him? If you execute a kick too slow or too fast, and your opponent moves, how are you going to hit him? If you attempt to execute a kick and your opponent is too close to you and jams the kick, how are your going to hit him? These are just a few of the problems that can be solved by creating the proper distance between you and your opponent and the utilization of proper timing. You cannot leave it up to chance or fate to create the perfect kicking distance between you and your opponent; you have to control the distance, and therefore the fight. Don't allow your opponent that opportunity.

Impact:

Impact is the culmination of all of the other principles and techniques performed correctly, in order to generate the maximum amount of force, and to transfer that power into your opponent at the precise moment of impact. If any one technique or principle is neglected, or applied improperly, then you will not be able to produce the maximum amount of force upon impact that you are capable of.

Follow Through:

Proper follow through of the foot and leg after kicking is perhaps one of the most important movements you can make during the kicking sequence. To begin with, the faster your follow through is after striking your target, the more effective your kick is going to be. This is primarily due to the transfer of energy that is being delivered from your entire body through your leg and foot into the intended target at the moment of impact. The longer your striking implement is in contact with its target, the more energy that is reflected back into you rather than being transferred into the target.

Secondly, the longer you have your foot in the air, the longer it is going to take you to follow up with another technique. It also allows your opponent the opportunity to grab your foot or leg and put you in a world of hurt. Unlike the movies where an actor can kick ten opponents all at once and never put his foot back on the ground, you should never attempt such a foolish stunt. Multiple kicks with one leg in the air can be effective, but only after years and years of devoted practice, and a cooperative opponent. As a general rule-of-thumb, as fast as your kick leaves the ground, it should be just as fast if not faster getting back down on the ground.

Visualization:

"Any sport is 95 percent mental, and anyone who tells you differently, doesn't know what he's talking about," Joe Fields, center for the New York Jets.

"Mind is everything, muscles are pieces of rubber", Paavo Nurmi, Olympic Gold Medallist.

Like I stated before, your mind controls your body. Therefore you have to believe in yourself and your abilities, if you ever want to become more proficient than what you currently are. There are three separate and unique times that one should utilize visualization as an effective training tool. They are; before, during and after every practice.

Before:

When you use visualization before practice you want to envision yourself performing the fastest, most powerful, most technically perfect kick you have ever done. Do not envision anything other than perfection. If you see yourself making mistakes or performing a kick poorly, then you will. If you see yourself doing your best then you will do your best. This is also referred to as positive thinking. It works, so use it. This should take anywhere from 5 to 15 minutes.

During:

As you are performing the kick, envision an imaginary target in front of you that you want to kick. Aim your kick to hit a certain target. Be aware of your body movement and position throughout the entire kicking sequence. Imagine your target being totally devastated by your kick. Concentrate.

After:

Use this time to reflect upon your workout and how well you did. Envision yourself doing even better the next time you practice. Answer this question, "If you don't believe in you, who will?"

24

Note: As I have demonstrated in the illustration below, an Out-to-In Axe Kick is executed almost identically to a lumberjack chopping a block of wood with an axe. However, instead of using an axe to chop a block of wood, you are using your foot to chop down an opponent. As you look at the illustration below, you can see that I swing the axe up (1) and around my right hand side (2) in a counterclockwise (clockwise from your perspective) motion until the axe reaches its "Peak of Arc" (3), which is when I change direction and bring the axe straight down in front of me and through the block of wood (4).

Out-to-In Axe Kick

The Axe Kick is one of the ten primary kicks associated with Karate and/or Tae Kwon Do. Although it goes by many different names, the Axe Kick, when performed and utilized properly, is one of the most powerful kicks in the martial artist's arsenal. This section will go into minute detail over all areas and phases of the Out-to-In Axe Kick. Once this co-primary kick is mastered, all of the other variations of this co-primary kick will fall into place. Without any further ado, let's get started.

Fighting Stance:

Your fighting stance should be approximately shoulder width apart (1a) with the toes of your front or lead foot pointed directly at your opponent. The heel of your lead foot should be in a direct line (1b) with the heel of your rear foot. This allows you the opportunity to initiate a faster kick. Remember that the foot positions in this stance will actually change after you become comfortable executing this kick. At that time your feet will still be approximately shoulder width apart in length, however the heels will be about 4 to 8 inches apart, rather than in a straight line with one another.

The toes of your back or rear foot (1b) should be pointed away from your body at a 45-degree angle. For example, if your right foot were in the rear position, then the toes of that foot would be pointed to the right at a 45-degree angle. If the left foot were in the rear position, then the toes of your left foot would be pointed to the left at a 45-degree angle.

Your weight should be distributed over the balls of both feet and not over the entire surface are of the feet. This way your mobility is increased and you will be able to facilitate a faster turn when executing the kick. The weight distribution over your feet should be approximately 55% over the lead leg and 45% over the rear leg. This also allows for faster movement when kicking or when evading your opponent's attack.

Your knees (2) should be slightly but not noticeably bent. The lead leg knee should be slightly bent over the lead leg foot in the direction of the toes. The same also holds true for the rear knee in the fact that it too should be slightly bent over the rear foot in the direction of the rear toes. The bending of the knees contributes to faster movement with the legs as they are not locked straight or rigid and have better mobility when slightly bent rather than straight.

Your body (3) is facing at a 45-degree angle to your opponent. This presents a smaller target area facing toward your opponent. It also allows you better mobility moving forward toward your opponent, or backward away from your opponent. Additionally it allows you quicker access to off-set your opponent by moving in the direction your body is facing.

Your hands (4a) and elbows (4b), should be held up like a boxer's, that is with the lead hand held up at head level and away from your face about 8 to 12 inches (toward your opponent). Your lead elbow should be tucked in along your side in order to protect your ribs and stomach area. Your rear hand is held up alongside your cheek or neck, with the palm of that hand facing toward your cheek. Your rear elbow is also tucked in along your side in order to protect your ribs and stomach area.

Your back (5) should be straight but not rigid and your lead shoulder should be raised up slightly in order to protect your chin.

Your head (6) is facing toward your opponent with the chin tucked down behind your upraised lead shoulder.

Your eyes (7) should focus like a flashlight on your opponent's chest to center your vision. At the same time, allow your peripheral vision to scan the rest of your opponent's body and therefore any movements he will make. A word of caution, **do not** become fixated on a particular spot or point of focus on your opponent. This becomes more of a hindrance than an asset when fighting.

Additionally, you should **never** take your eyes off your opponent for any reason. This mistake is quite common when first learning how to kick. A lot of students tend to watch their foot as it travels from the floor to its intended target. This is not only incorrect, but it can be very dangerous! Always maintain proper eye contact with your opponent. Remember the old saying, "Look before you leap?"

Fighting Position Foot Position
(Beginning)

Fighting Position Foot Position
(Advanced)

Note: To better understand the visual aspects of an Out-to-In Axe Kick, imagine that you have a "front view" and that you are looking at yourself standing in front of the protractor image which is shown on the right. In a "Fighting Position," your base leg (0), which in this case is your left leg, is at the 0-degree position, while your kicking leg (1), in this case the right leg, is at approximately the 15-degree position.

Front View

27

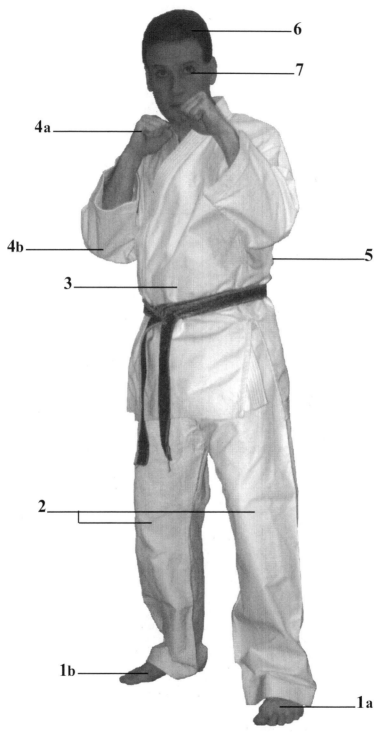

Fighting Position Front View

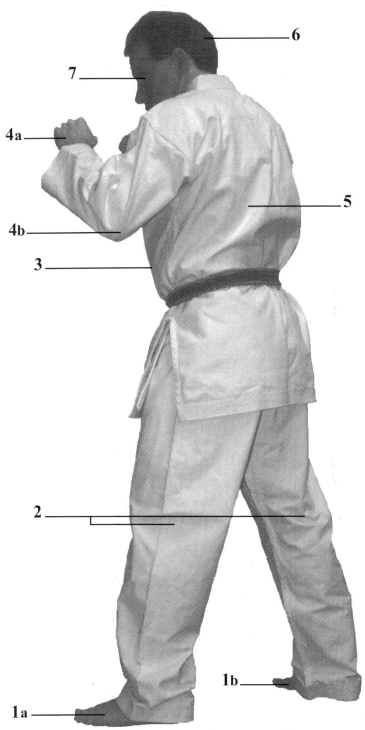

Fighting Position Side View

Begin Arc:

Shifting your weight onto your base leg foot (8), while simultaneously utilizing the toes of your kicking foot (11), push off the floor and bring your kicking leg up at approximately a 45-degree angle to your right (your opponents left), while keeping your kicking leg and knee (10) straight, but not locked. This will place 100% of your weight onto your base leg. As soon as your kicking foot leaves the ground, it should already be in the correct position to strike your opponent. As your kicking leg begins its upward "Path of Trajectory," your upper body (12a) should start turning in a counterclockwise direction so that the front of your body (12a) will be facing towards your opponent. Be sure and keep your back (12b) as straight as possible, but not rigid. Your base leg foot (8) is going to temporarily remain pointed directly at your opponent, while your base leg knee (9) remains slightly bent. However, immediately after you begin to execute this kick, you will pivot approximately 45-degrees counterclockwise, in which your base leg foot will remain in that position until after the delivery and subsequent "Follow Through" of the Axe Kick.

*Begin Arc
Foot Position*

Your hands (13a) and elbows (13b) should still be in relatively the same position as they were in fighting position. That is like a boxer's with the lead hand held up at head level and away from your face about 8 to 12 inches (toward your opponent). Your lead elbow should be tucked in along your side in order to protect your ribs and stomach area. Your rear hand is held up alongside your cheek or neck, with the palm of that hand facing toward your cheek. Your rear elbow is also tucked in along your side in order to protect your ribs and stomach area.

Your back (12b) should be straight and facing away from your opponent. You should not be hunched over or bent forward at the waist.

Your head (14) is facing straight ahead, and focused on your opponent's chest like a flashlight, not a laser beam. Your chin is tucked down behind your base leg shoulder, and your eyes (15) should still be centered on your opponent's chest.

Note: Maintaining the same visual perspective as you had in the previous illustration on page 27, and in the following illustrations on pages 33 and 36, imagine that you are beginning to execute the Out-to-In Axe Kick. Begin by raising your kicking leg from the "Fighting Position" (1) at approximately the 15-degree position, to the "Begin Arc" position (2), which is located at approximately the 70-degree position. While your base leg (0) remains at the 0-degree position.

Front View

Begin Arc Front View

Begin Arc Side View

3/4 to Peak of Arc:

As your kicking leg and foot continue along their upward "Path of Trajectory," your base foot (16) which now bears 100% of your weight after shifting the weight onto it in order to begin execution of the kick, should now pivot approximately 45-degrees counterclockwise by pivoting on the ball of the foot.

3/4 to Peak of Arc Foot Position

The base leg knee (17) remains slightly bent in the direction of the toes of the base foot. Your kicking leg and foot (19) has now moved up to your opponent's head height by continuing along the upward "Path of Trajectory," while maintaining approximately a 45-degree angle to your right (your opponents left). Your toes should be flexed towards your kicking leg knee, so that with your leg extended, your heel will strike the target rather than your toes or sole of your foot. Your kicking leg and knee (18) should remain straight, but not locked. Once your kicking foot (19) has left the ground, it should remain in the correct striking position throughout the entire kick until returning back to the ground. After your foot has left the ground, the muscles in your thigh contract to bring your leg up into the "Peak of Arc" position.

Your upper body (20a) should now be facing directly towards your opponent. Your back (20b) should remain straight, but not rigid, while leaning back slightly.

Too many martial artists are sacrificing a proper upward "Path of Trajectory" in order to get the kick to the "Peak of Arc" and therefore, to the target faster. Although it is true to a certain extent that a kick will get to the "Peak of Arc" and therefore, to the target faster without utilizing the correct upward "Path of Trajectory," it is incorrect and can prove potentially harmful to the individual kicker. Proper technique should never be sacrificed for the sake of speed.

Your hands (21a) and elbows (21b), are also in relatively the same position as in (13a) and (13b), although they will occasionally change position to coincide with the various changes in body position, which take place throughout the execution of this kick. Your head (22) remains in the same position as in (14). Your eyes (23) are still focused on your opponent's chest like a flashlight, not a laser beam.

Note: As your kicking leg continues along its upward "Path of Trajectory," it will have moved from the "Begin Arc" position (2), to the "3/4 to Peak of Arc" position (3), which is located at approximately the 140-degree position. Although you will be pivoting on the ball of your base leg foot, your base leg (0) should remain at the 0-degree position.

Front View

33

Upward Path of Trajectory

22
23
21a
19
21b
20b
18
20a
17
16

3/4 to Peak of Arc Front View

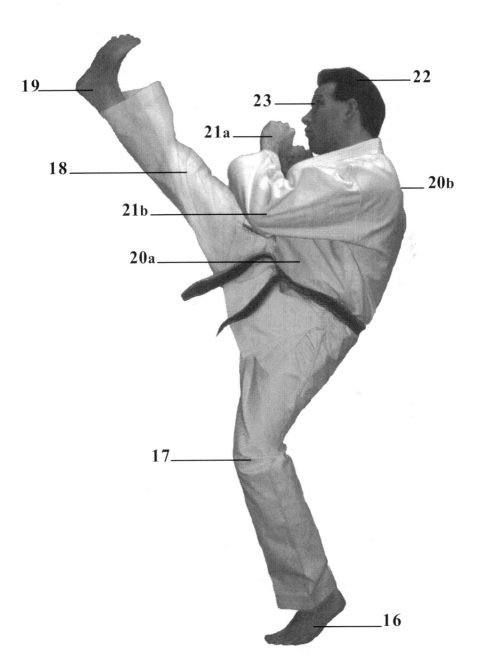

3/4 to Peak of Arc Side View

Peak of Arc:

Your base foot (24) remains in approximately the same position as in (16). Your base leg knee (25) is still slightly bent as you reach the "Peak of Arc." Your kicking leg and knee remain straight (but not locked), as they have now moved up to the correct height and position in order to begin their downward "Path of Trajectory." In this position, your kicking leg from your hip all the way up to your kicking leg heel (27), should be in a straight vertical line and flush against your upper torso and chest (28a). The toes of your kicking foot (27) are pointed directly behind you and flexed back toward your knee in order to fully expose the heel of your kicking foot as the striking implement. Although your toes and foot are flexed towards the kicking leg knee, do not flex them to the point of having your foot and ankle too tight. It should be a relaxed tension or flexion.

Peak of Arc
Foot Position

When looking at the downward "Path of Trajectory" from the front view, the heel of your kicking foot (27) will follow a straight line of trajectory from the "Peak of Arc" through the target (Impact) and continuing through to the "Follow Through" position. However, when you look at the downward "Path of Trajectory" from the side view, the heel of your kicking foot appears to be traveling in a crescent type motion. This is correct.

Your upper body (28a) should now be facing at a slight angle towards your opponent, with the kicking leg side of your body closer to your opponent than your base leg side. Your back (28b) remains straight but not rigid, and is facing away from your opponent, while continuing to lean back slightly.

Your hands (29a), and elbows (29b), are still in relatively the same position as previously described during the initial "Fighting Position." That is like a boxer's, with your hands up high around your chest and chin, and your elbows along side your rib cage.

Your head (30) remains facing directly toward your opponent with your chin tucked down into your chest. Your eyes (31) should be looking straight ahead, and focused on your opponent's chest.

Note: Your kicking leg will have continued its upward "Path of Trajectory" and has now moved the remaining 40-degrees from the "3/4 to Peak of Arc" position (3), to the "Peak of Arc" position (4), which is located at the 180-degree position. Although you will be pivoting on the ball of your base leg foot, your base leg (0) should remain at the 0-degree position.

Note: During the downward "Path of Trajectory," your kicking foot will travel in a straight line from the "Peak of Arc" (4) all the way down to the "Follow Through" position (0).

Front View

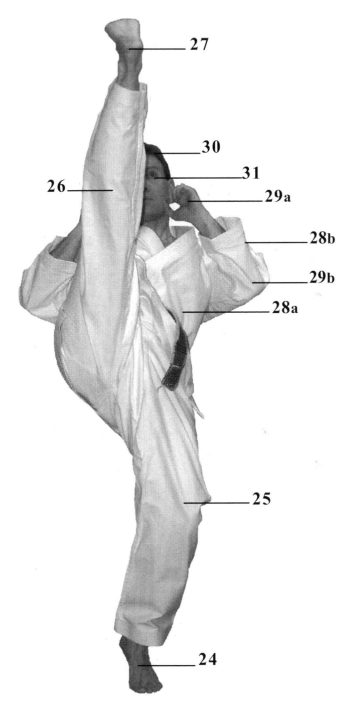

27

30

31

26

29a

28b

29b

28a

25

24

Peak of Arc Front View

37

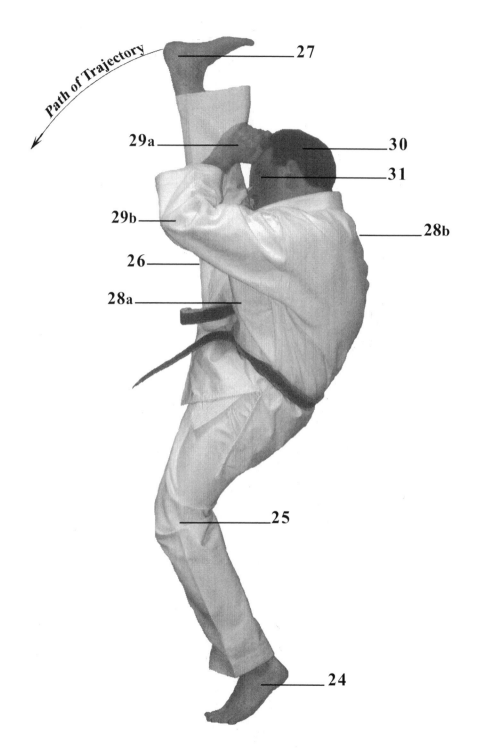

Path of Trajectory

27

29a

30

31

29b

28b

26

28a

25

24

Peak of Arc Side View

Impact:
Your entire base leg foot (32) should now be in contact with the ground, while simultaneously gripping the floor with the entire foot. In other words, your entire foot should be in solid contact with the ground with the toes still pointed at a 45-degree angle to your left (your opponents right). Your base leg knee (33) is now straightened slightly, but not locked, at the moment of impact to add power to the kick.

Impact
Foot Position

The heel of your kicking foot (35), with the toes pulled back and towards your kicking knee, should now be making contact with the appropriate, vital or vulnerable point, in one of the selected target areas on your opponent. Remember that the contact time between your striking implement and the opponent's target area is minimal. Do not push the technique to the target area and then let it hang in the air. Explosively strike through the target and get your foot back down on the ground!

At the moment of impact, your entire kicking leg from the heel (35) to the hips, along with your back (36b), shoulders, and head (38), should be in alignment while the entire body tightens immediately upon impact with the target, and then relaxes again, in order to facilitate a faster follow through. In order to help prevent injury, at the moment of impact, there should be a slight bend in your kicking leg knee (34).

Your upper body (36a), should still be facing at a slight angle towards your opponent, with the kicking leg side of your body closer to your opponent than your base leg side. Your back (36b) remains straight but not rigid, and is facing away from your opponent, while continuing to lean back slightly.

Your hands (37a) and elbows (37b), should still be up in relatively the same position as before in (29a) and (29b). Do not let them fly all over like a bird flapping its wings. Keep the elbows in to protect the rib cage and your hands up to protect your head.

Your head (38) is still facing towards your opponent with the chin tucked down into your chest. Your eyes (39) should still be looking straight ahead, and focused on your opponent's chest.

Note: To better understand the visual aspects of an Out-to-In Axe Kick from the "Peak of Arc" position to the "Return to Fighting Position," imagine that you have a "side view" and that you are looking at yourself standing in front of the protractor image which is shown on the right. Your kicking leg, which has completed its upward "Path of Trajectory," will now travel along its downward "Path of Trajectory" from the "Peak of Arc" position (5) approximately 40-degrees where it will make initial contact with your opponent at the "Impact" position (6). Your base leg (0) should remain at the 0-degree position.

Side View

39

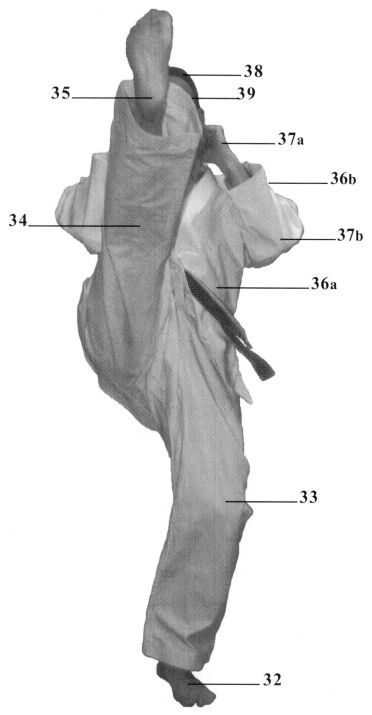

38

35

39

37a

36b

34

37b

36a

33

32

Impact Front View

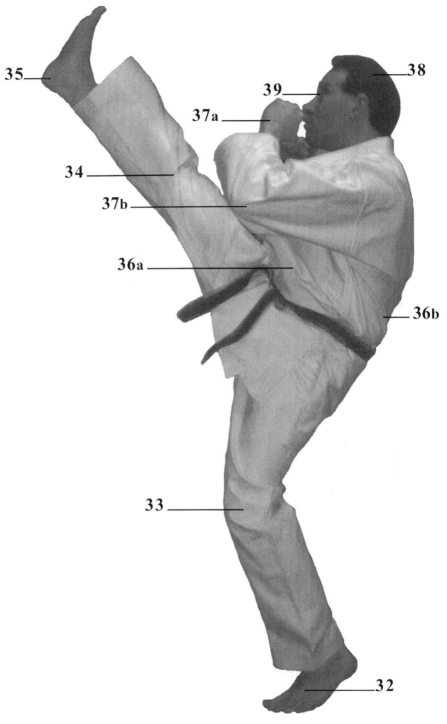

Impact Side View

Follow Through:

Your entire base leg foot (40) should remain in contact with the ground, while simultaneously gripping the floor with the entire foot. In other words, your entire foot should be in solid contact with the ground with the toes still pointed at a 45-degree angle to your left (your opponents right). Your base leg knee (41) although straight, should have a slight bend in it. The kicking leg knee (42) remains straight, but not locked. While your kicking foot (43), which should have continued along the same downward "Path of Trajectory" from the "Peak of Arc"

Follow Through Foot Position

to "Impact," should be straight in front of you at approximately the height of your base leg knee (41). The toes on your kicking foot (43) should remain flexed back towards your kicking leg knee. Although they will begin to relax as they move from this position back down to the ground.

Too many martial artists seem to have a tendency to leave their kicks "hanging" in the air after executing a kick, rather than completing their kicks and returning them back down to the ground. My instructors used to call this "posing your kicks." This is an **extremely bad habit** to get into and one that needs to be corrected immediately.

Always remember, that your kicking foot should travel from the target back to its original starting position just as fast, if not faster, than it did from its initial fighting position to the target.

Your upper body (44a) should still be facing at a slight angle towards your opponent, with the kicking leg side of your body closer to your opponent than your base leg side. Your back (44b) remains straight but not rigid, and is facing away from your opponent, while continuing to lean back slightly.

Your hands (45a) and elbows (45b), are also in relatively the same position as they were in (37a) and (37b).

Your head (46) remains in relatively the same position that it has been in throughout the entire kick. Your eyes (47), if you executed the kick properly, should be still be on your opponent, although they may not be focused on your opponent's chest if you have knocked him down. **Never take your eyes off of your opponent.**

Note: Maintaining the same visual perspective as you had in the previous illustration on page 39, and in the following illustrations on page 49, imagine that you have just made initial contact with your opponent at the "Impact" point (6), and have continued to strike through your opponent. Your kicking foot will continue to travel along its downward "Path of Trajectory" approximately 70-degrees to the "Follow Through" position (7). While your base leg (0) continues to remain at the 0-degree position.

Side View

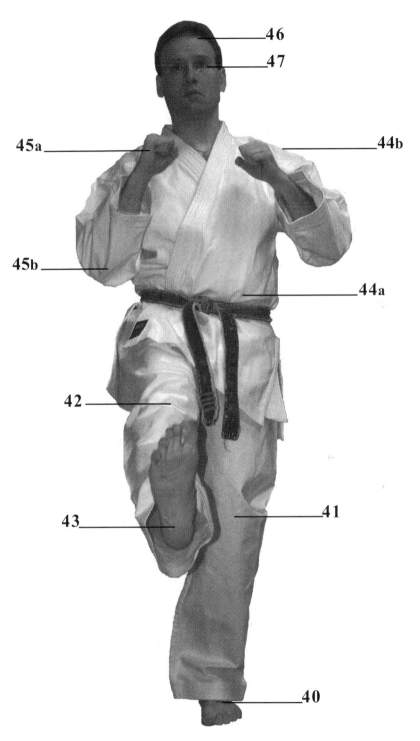

46

47

45a

44b

45b

44a

42

41

43

40

Follow Through Front View

43

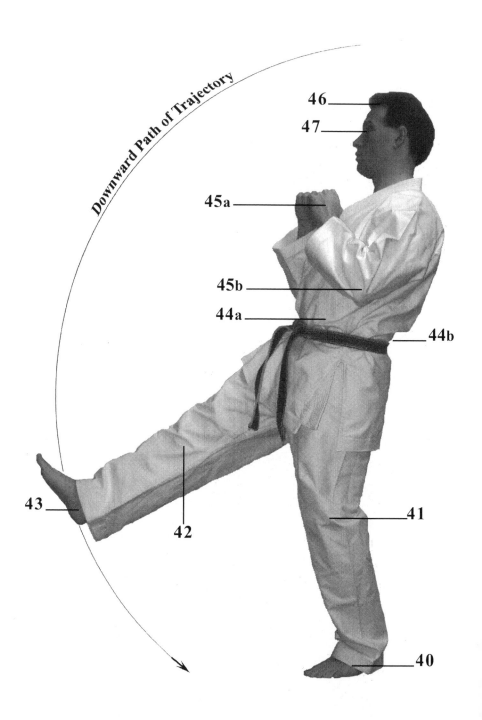

Downward Path of Trajectory

46

47

45a

45b

44a

44b

43

42

41

40

Follow Through Side View

Return to Fighting Position #1:

After you have reached the "Follow Through" position, pivot 45-degrees clockwise (if kicking with the right leg, counter-clockwise if you are kicking with the left leg) by pivoting on the ball of your base leg foot, and returning your kicking foot back to its original starting position. Your head, shoulders and hips will all come back around to your original fighting position before your kicking leg foot touches the ground. Your entire body should be upright and straight although not rigid throughout the entire return to your original fighting position.

Position #1

Once you return to Fighting Position, your fighting stance should once again be approximately shoulder width apart (48a) with the toes of your front or lead foot pointed directly at your opponent. The heel of your lead foot should be in a direct line (48b) with the heel of your rear foot. The toes of your back or rear foot (48b) should be pointed away from your body at a 45-degree angle. For example, if your right foot were in the rear position, then the toes of that foot would be pointed to the right at a 45-degree angle. If the left foot were in the rear position, then the toes of your left foot would be pointed to the left at a 45-degree angle.

Your weight should once again be distributed over the balls of both feet and not over the entire surface are of the feet. The weight distribution over your feet should be approximately 55% over the lead leg and 45% over the rear leg.

Your knees (49) should be slightly but not noticeably bent. The lead leg knee should be slightly bent over the lead leg foot in the direction of the toes. The same also holds true for the rear knee in the fact that it too should be slightly bent over the rear foot in the direction of the rear toes. The bending of the knees contributes to faster movement with the legs as they are not locked straight or rigid and have better mobility when slightly bent rather than straight.

Your body (50) is facing at a 45-degree angle to your opponent. Your hands (51a) and elbows (51b), should still be held up like a boxer's, that is with the lead hand held up at head level and away from your face about 8 to 12 inches (toward your opponent). Your lead elbow should be tucked in along your side in order to protect your ribs and stomach area. Your rear hand is held up alongside your cheek with the palm of that hand facing toward your cheek. Your rear elbow is also tucked in along your side in order to protect your ribs and stomach area.

Your back (52) should be straight but not rigid and your lead shoulder should be raised up slightly in order to protect your chin.

Your head (53) is facing toward your opponent with the chin tucked down behind your upraised lead shoulder. Your eyes (54) should focus like a flashlight on the chest or center of your opponent whether he is still standing or not. At the same time, allow your peripheral vision to scan the rest of your opponent's body and therefore any movements he will make. I cannot stress this enough, **do not** become fixated on a particular spot or point of focus on your opponent. This becomes more of a hindrance than an asset when fighting.

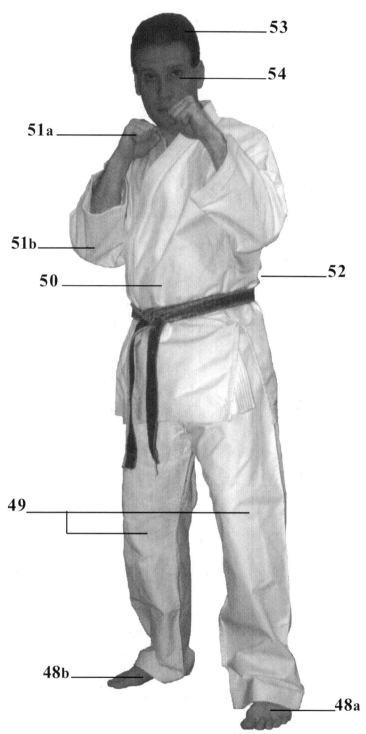

Return to Fighting Position #1 Front View

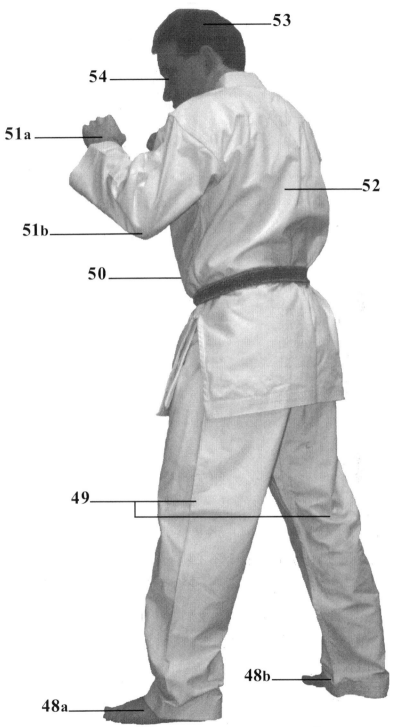

Return to Fighting Position #1 Side View

47

Return to Fighting Position #2:

After you have reached the "Follow Through" position, simply set your kicking foot down in front of you and toward your opponent, with your kicking leg in the forward position rather than in the rearward position. Your head, shoulders and hips will all move into another fighting position before your kicking leg foot touches the ground in front of you.

Your entire body should be upright and straight although not rigid throughout the entire return to your new fighting position. Remember that by stepping forward after this kick, you may be putting yourself in a more dangerous position because you are stepping in toward your opponent, which will put you closer to him. Be extra cautious when executing this move.

Position #2

Once you return to a Fighting Position, your fighting stance should once again be approximately shoulder width apart (55a) with the toes of your front or lead foot pointed directly at your opponent. The heel of your lead foot should be in a direct line (55b) with the heel of your rear foot. The toes of your back or rear foot (55b) should be pointed away from your body at a 45-degree angle. For example, if your left foot were in the rear position, then the toes of that foot would be pointed to the left at a 45-degree angle. If the right foot were in the rear position, then the toes of your right foot would be pointed to the right at a 45-degree angle.

Your weight should once again be distributed over the balls of both feet and not over the entire surface are of the feet. The weight distribution over your feet should be approximately 55% over the lead leg and 45% over the rear leg.

Your knees (56) should be slightly but not noticeably bent. The lead leg knee should be slightly bent over the lead leg foot in the direction of the toes. The same also holds true for the rear knee in the fact that it too should be slightly bent over the rear foot in the direction of the rear toes. The bending of the knees contributes to faster movement with the legs as they are not locked straight or rigid and have better mobility when slightly bent rather than straight.

Your body (57) is facing at a 45-degree angle to your opponent. Your hands (58a) and elbows (58b), should still be held up like a boxer's, that is with the lead hand held up at head level and away from your face about 8 to 12 inches (toward your opponent). Your lead elbow should be tucked in along your side in order to protect your ribs and stomach area. Your rear hand is held up alongside your cheek with the palm of that hand facing toward your cheek. Your rear elbow is also tucked in along your side in order to protect your ribs and stomach area.

Your back (59) should be straight but not rigid and your lead shoulder should be raised up slightly in order to protect your chin.

Your head (60) is facing toward your opponent with the chin tucked down behind your upraised lead shoulder. Your eyes (61) should focus like a flashlight on the chest or center of your opponent whether he is still standing or not. At the same time, allow your peripheral vision to scan the rest of your opponent's body and therefore any movements he will make.

Note: If you paid close attention to the photographs from the "3/4 to Peak of Arc" position to "Impact," you will see that I have intentionally demonstrated one of the most common mistakes that is made when executing an Axe Kick. That is executing the kick while balancing on the ball of your base leg foot. This is incorrect! Your entire base leg foot should always remain in total contact with the ground at the moment of impact. The only time you should be balancing on the ball of your base leg foot, is when you are pivoting to get into the proper foot position in order to deliver your kick in the most effective and efficient manner possible.

Note: In the "Return to Fighting Position #1," your kicking foot will travel approximately 85-degrees from the "Follow Through" position (7) back to its original starting position (8). While your base leg (0) continues to remain at the 0-degree position.

Note: In the "Return to Fighting Position #2," your kicking foot will travel approximately 55-degrees from the "Follow Through" position (7) to another "Fighting Position" (9). However, this time you have stepped forward with your kicking leg rather than returning it to its original starting position as I have illustrated for you above. Your base leg (0) continues to remain at the 0-degree position, although now it will be in the rearward rather than the forward position.

49

Return to Fighting Position #2 Front View

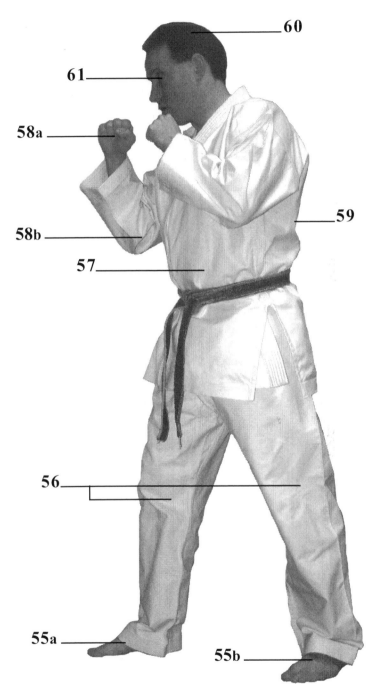

60

61

58a

59

58b

57

56

55a

55b

Return to Fighting Position #2 Side View

51

Pictorial Overview:

Fighting Position

Begin Arc

3/4 to Peak of Arc

Peak of Arc

Impact

Follow Through

Position #1

Position #2

52

Note: The illustration below is a visual overview from a "front" perspective of the upward "Path of Trajectory" that your kicking foot will take from the initial "Fighting Position" to the "Peak of Arc" position when executing an Out-to-In Axe Kick with the right leg.

0. The position of your base leg throughout the execution of the entire kick from start to finish is at the 0-degree position.
1. The position of your kicking leg in its initial "Fighting Position" is at the 15-degree position.
2. The position of your kicking leg as it moves along its upward "Path of Trajectory" approximately 55-degrees to the "Begin Arc" position at the 70-degree position.
3. The position of your kicking leg as it continues along its upward "Path of Trajectory" approximately 70-degrees more to the "3.4 to Peak of Arc" position at the 140-degree position.
4. The position of your kicking leg as it reaches the "Peak of Arc" position which should be at the 180-degree position.

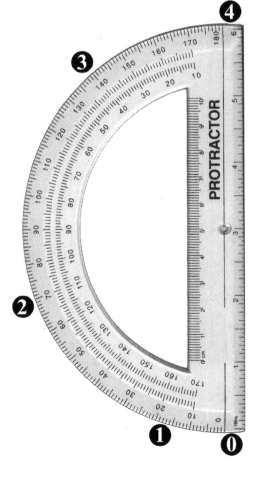

Note: The illustration below is a visual overview from a "side" perspective of the downward "Path of Trajectory" that your kicking foot will take from the "Peak of Arc" position to either one of the two "Return to Fighting Positions" when executing either an Out-to-In Axe Kick or a In-to-Out Axe Kick. This illustration is the same for both the right and left leg.

0. The position of your base leg throughout the execution of the entire kick from start to finish is at the 0-degree position.
5. The position of your kicking leg at the "Peak of Arc" position at the 180-degree position.
6. The position of your kicking leg as it moves along its downward "Path of Trajectory" approximately 40-degrees to the "Impact" position at the 140-degree position.
7. The position of your kicking leg as it continues along its downward "Path of Trajectory" and through its target approximately 70-degrees more to the "Follow Through" position at the 70-degree position.
8. The position of your kicking leg as it returns to its initial "Fighting Position" at the (negative) 15-degree position.
9. The position of your kicking leg if you set it down in front of you instead of behind you in its original starting position.

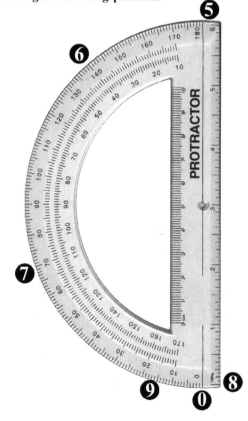

54

Variations of the Out-to-In Axe Kick

This chapter will explain in detail how to properly execute five variations of the Out-to-In Axe Kick. Remember that all of these variations are derived from the co-primary kick Out-to-In Axe Kick. Therefore, it is essential that you learn Out-to-In Axe Kick first before attempting any of these other variations.

To perhaps give you a better understanding of what I mean, let me use the comparison of building a house. Before you start building your house you are first going to need a set of blueprints, this would be the equivalent of the material presented in this book. Next you are going to need the proper materials to begin building with, this would be the equivalent of properly warming-up and stretching before you attempt to practice these kicks.

Next comes the hardest part for students to understand, now in order for your house to be stable, sturdy, and secure you must first have a very well built and strong foundation. The foundation of your house is made out of concrete, while the foundation of this particular type of kick is, the Out-to-In Axe Kick. Once you have a strong and proficient Out-to-In Axe Kick, then you can begin to build upon that with the many different variations of that kick. Just like you would build your frame, walls, ceilings, floors, and roof of your house.

If you don't take the time to first build a strong and stable foundation, your kicking skills along with your house, will not last and will collapse when the first strong storm or self-defense situation comes along.

As a general rule of thumb, every time you practice one of the variations of Out-to-In Axe Kick, you should practice Out-to-In Axe Kick itself at least ten times. I promise you that if you do this, all of your Axe Kicks will steadily improve and become stronger.

Back Spin Out-to-In Axe Kick

The Back Spin Out-to-In Axe Kick is identical in execution to the Out-to-In Axe Kick, with one notable exception. A back spinning forward motion, which is performed immediately prior to executing the kick. This back spinning forward motion is used to "close the distance" between you and your opponent, and when used properly, to misdirect or deceive your opponent in order to increase your chances of successfully executing the kick. It can also increase the power in this kick due to the added momentum of back spinning forward. The actual back spinning forward motion is performed by pivoting counterclockwise on the ball of your lead foot when kicking with the right leg (clockwise when kicking with the left leg), and bringing your rear leg forward into another fighting position. The distance covered when you back spin forward, should be approximately one shoulder width. Keep your hips and upper body as still as possible throughout the initial back spin forward in order to avoid telegraphing the move to your opponent.

Fighting Position:

1. Your fighting position for this kick is exactly the same as it will be for Switch Axe Kick. With your kicking leg in the forward position to begin with rather than in the rearward position.

2. This stance is approximately shoulder width apart with the heel of your rear foot in a direct line with the heel of your front foot.

3. Your front or lead foot should be pointing directly at your opponent.

4. Your rear foot is angled toward the left at approximately a 45-degree angle. Your weight should be distributed evenly over the balls of both feet.

5. Your knees are slightly, but not noticeably bent. They should not be locked straight or rigid.

6. Your body should be facing at a 45-degree angle toward your opponent. This presents a smaller target area and also facilitates a faster back-spin forward and turn, which allows you the opportunity to initiate a faster kick.

7. Your hands should be held up (like a boxers), with the elbows tucked in to protect the ribs and your hands up to protect your head. Your hands should remain as close to this position as possible throughout the entire kick.

8. Your head should be facing your opponent with your chin tucked down and protected by your lead shoulder.

9. Your eyes should be centered on your opponent's chest.

Fighting Position
Foot Position

Fighting Position Front View

Fighting Position Side View

56

Back Spin & Step Forward:

10. Pivoting on the ball of your lead leg foot, turn counterclockwise and step forward with your rear foot approximately your shoulder width into another fighting position. As you are moving your rear foot forward, be sure and keep your weight centered over your lead leg. Also, don't make a big sweeping motion with your rear foot as you move it forward, keep it in close to your base leg foot as you turn. This helps maintain your balance while giving you a direct line of trajectory to your target.

11. As you execute the back spin, your back will momentarily be facing directly toward your opponent at approximately the midway point in the back spin. As you are completing the back spin forward, you will begin to execute the kick.

12. While you are back spinning forward, you should be turning your head and looking over your back spinning (non-kicking) leg shoulder. This will enable you to maintain eye contact with your opponent throughout the entire movement.

Back Spin & Step Forward Foot Position

Note: In order to avoid unnecessary knee injuries when kicking, always pivot on the ball of your foot, not the heel.

Back Spin & Step Forward Front View   *Back Spin & Step Forward Side View*

Turn & Begin Arc:

13. When the ball of your base leg foot touches the ground, utilize the toes of your kicking foot and push off the floor bringing your kicking leg up at approximately a 45-degree angle to your opponents left. Your leg should be straight, and your kicking foot should already be in the correct position to strike your opponent.

14. As your bring your kicking leg up, your upper body should start turning as it begins to face towards your opponent. Your back will remain straight but not rigid.

15. Your head is up and facing towards your opponent, while your eyes remain in contact with your opponent throughout the entire kick.

16. Although your hands have switched position, they should still be held up (like a boxer's), with the elbows tucked in to protect the ribs and your hands up to protect your head.

Begin Arc
Foot Position

Note: The first half of the "back spin" motion can be likened to the "coiling" up of a high tension spring. While the second half of the "back spin" motion, as the ball of your base leg foot touches the ground after "back spinning" and stepping forward, releases the spring resulting in your body rapidly and explosively completing the "back spin" while simultaneously initiating the kick.

Turn & Begin Arc Front View   *Turn & Begin Arc Side View*

3/4 to Peak of Arc:

17. Your base leg foot should now have moved approximately 45-degrees (counterclockwise) by pivoting on the ball of your foot, while the knee on your base leg remains slightly bent. Your kicking leg has now moved up to your opponent's head height, although still at a 45-degree angle to your opponents left.

3/4 to Peak of Arc Foot Position

18. Your kicking foot remains in the correct striking position throughout the entire sequence.
19. Your upper body is now facing towards your opponent and leaning back slightly.
20. Although your body is in the above position, your back remains straight but not rigid, and your head should still be facing towards your opponent. Your eyes should continue to remain in contact with your opponent throughout the entire kick.

Note: Throughout the entire kicking sequence, you can see that my arms are held up and close to my body, they are not flapping around like a bird. However, if you look at the photograph on the left, you will see that my left arm is out a bit further from my body than it should be. If you find yourself doing this, remember that it is incorrect and a quite common mistake that many martial artists make when kicking. Remember to keep your arms up and close to your body.

3/4 to Peak of Arc Front View

3/4 to Peak of Arc Side View

59

Peak of Arc:

21. Your base leg foot should still be in approximately the same position, with your base leg knee being slightly bent. Your kicking leg has now moved up to the correct height to begin its downward trajectory.

22. The heel of the kicking foot should follow a straight line of trajectory from the "Peak of Arc" through the target (Impact), to the "Follow Through" position.

23. Your upper body should now be facing at a slight angle towards your opponent, while continuing to lean back slightly. In this position, the kicking leg side of your body will be closer to your opponent than your base leg side.

24. Although your body is in the above position, your back remains straight but not rigid, and your head should still be facing towards your opponent. Eye contact with your opponent is maintained at all times.

Peak of Arc Foot Position

Note: In order to effectively utilize this kick in a tournament or self-defense situation, you must have developed a very high degree of flexibility not only in your legs, but also in your hips and lower back. Stretching should be performed not only before and after every workout, but also first thing in the morning when you get up and periodically throughout the day.

Peak of Arc Front View

Peak of Arc Side View

Impact:

25. Your entire base leg foot should now be in contact with the ground and gripping it, while in approximately the same position.

26. Your upper body, with the kicking leg side of your body remaining closer to your opponent than your base leg side, should still be facing at a slight angle towards your opponent, while continuing to lean back slightly. At the moment of impact, your entire body should tighten to add power to the kick, as your foot continues to travel on a downward trajectory through the target.

27. Notice how your kicking foot, kicking leg, hips, back, shoulders and head are all in alignment at the initial moment of "Impact." Also, notice how the toes of the kicking foot are pulled back towards your body and pointed up. This helps insure that contact with the target is made with the back of the heel.

28. Your head should still be facing towards your opponent. Eye contact with your opponent is maintained at all times.

Impact Foot Position

Note: **A lot of martial artists have the misconception that an Axe Kick is only used to the head of a standing opponent, this is not true! An Axe Kick is actually more effective against an opponent who is bent over, or even already lying on the ground.**

Impact Front View

Impact Side View

61

Follow Through:

29. Your entire base leg foot should remain in contact with the ground and gripping it, while in approximately the same position. The knee on your base leg will remain slightly bent.

30. Your upper body, with the kicking leg side of your body remaining closer to your opponent than your base leg side, should still be facing at a slight angle towards your opponent, while continuing to lean back slightly.

Follow Through Foot Position

31. Your kicking leg foot should continue along exactly the same downward path it followed from the "Peak of Arc" to "Impact." Your foot should now be at approximately knee level.

32. Your head should still be facing towards your opponent. Eye contact with your opponent is maintained at all times.

Note: Would you screw a screw into a piece of wood with a saw? Would you cut a board with a screwdriver? Remember to use the correct tool for each particular situation. Kicking may be effective in one situation, but ineffective in another. An Axe Kick may be the correct kick to use in one kicking situation, but totally ineffective in another.

Follow Through Front View

Follow Through Side View

Return to Fighting Position:
There are two ways that you can return to a fighting position from the "Follow Through" position. They are as follows:

33a. After you have reached the "Follow Through" position, simply bring your kicking foot behind you and set it down into a fighting position with your kicking leg behind you, rather than in front of you.

Position #1

33b. After you have reached the "Follow Through" position, simply leave your kicking foot in front of you and set it down into a fighting position with your kicking leg in front of you, rather than behind you.

Position #2

Note: Whether or not you are kicking to the body or head, the same principle of **STRIKING THROUGH** the target, rather than merely striking the target surface still applies. However, you must keep in mind that the head moves a lot easier than the body, and is farther from the ground than the body. Which, generally speaking, means that it will take longer for a kick to get from the ground to the head, than from the ground to the body.

Pictorial Overview:

Fighting Position   *Back Spin & Step Forward*   *Turn & Begin Arc*

3/4 to Peak of Arc   *Peak of Arc*   *Impact*

Follow Through   *Position #1*   *Position #2*

Spin Back Out-to-In Axe Kick

The Spin Back Out-to-In Axe Kick is identical in execution to the Out-to-In Axe Kick, with one notable exception. A spinning backward motion, which is performed immediately prior to executing the kick. This spinning backward motion is used to draw your opponent in to you, or to avoid an attack, it is also used to misdirect or deceive your opponent in order to increase your chances of successfully executing the kick. This move can also increase the power in this kick due to the added momentum of spinning backward. The actual spinning backward motion is performed by pivoting counterclockwise on the ball of your rear foot when kicking with the right leg (clockwise when kicking with the left leg), and bringing your lead leg backward into another fighting position. The distance covered when you spin backward, should be approximately one shoulder width. Keep your hips and upper body as still as possible throughout the initial spin backward in order to avoid telegraphing the move to your opponent.

Fighting Position:
1. Your fighting position for this kick is exactly the same as it will be for Switch Axe Kick. With your kicking leg in the forward position to begin with rather than in the rearward position.
2. This stance is approximately shoulder width apart with the heel of your rear foot in a direct line with the heel of your front foot.
3. Your front or lead foot should be pointing directly at your opponent.

Fighting Position
Foot Position

Fighting Position Front View   *Fighting Position Side View*

65

4. Your rear foot is angled toward the left at approximately a 45-degree angle. Your weight should be distributed evenly over the balls of both feet.
5. Your knees are slightly, but not noticeably bent. They should not be locked straight or rigid.
6. Your body should be facing at a 45-degree angle toward your opponent. This presents a smaller target area and also facilitates a faster spin-back backward and turn, which allows you the opportunity to initiate a faster kick.
7. Your hands should be held up (like a boxers), with the elbows tucked in to protect the ribs and your hands up to protect your head. Your hands should remain as close to this position as possible throughout the entire kick.
8. Your head should be facing your opponent with your chin tucked down and protected by your lead shoulder.
9. Your eyes should be centered on your opponent's chest.

Spin Back & Step Backward:
10. Pivoting on the ball of your rear leg foot, turn counter-clockwise and step backward with your front foot approximately your shoulder width into another fighting position. As you are moving your front foot backward, be sure and keep your weight centered over your rear leg. Also, don't make a big sweeping motion with your front foot as you step backwards, keep it in

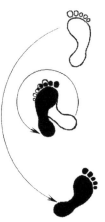

Spin Backward Foot Position

Spin Back & Step Backward Front View   *Spin Back & Step Backward Side View*

close to your base leg foot as you turn. This helps maintain your balance while giving you a direct line of trajectory to your target.

11. As you execute the spin back, your back will momentarily be facing directly toward your opponent at approximately the midway point in the spin back. As you are completing the spin back, you will begin to execute the kick.

12. While you are spinning backward, you should be turning your head and looking over your spinning backward (non-kicking) leg shoulder. This will enable you to maintain eye contact with your opponent throughout the entire movement.

Turn & Begin Arc:

13. Pivoting on the balls of your feet, complete the turn and using the toes of your kicking foot, push off the floor and bring your kicking leg up at approximately a 45-degree angle to your opponents left. Your leg should be straight, and your kicking foot should already be in the correct position to strike your opponent.

14. As your bring your kicking leg up, your upper body should start turning as it begins to face towards your opponent. Your back will remain straight but not rigid.

15. Although your hands have switched position, they should still be held up (like a boxer's), with the elbows in to protect the ribs and your hands up to protect your head.

16. Your head is up and facing towards your opponent, while your eyes remain in contact with your opponent throughout the entire kick.

*Begin Arc
Foot Position*

Turn & Begin Arc Front View   *Turn & Begin Arc Side View*

3/4 to Peak of Arc:

17. Your base leg foot should now have moved approximately 45-degrees (counterclockwise) by pivoting on the ball of your foot, while the knee on your base leg remains slightly bent. Your kicking leg has now moved up to your opponent's head height, although still at a 45-degree angle to your opponents left.

3/4 to Peak of Arc Foot Position

18. Your kicking foot remains in the correct striking position throughout the entire sequence.

19. Your upper body is now facing towards your opponent and leaning back slightly.

20. Although your body is in the above position, your back remains straight but not rigid, and your head should still be facing towards your opponent. Your eyes should continue to remain in contact with your opponent throughout the entire kick.

Note: Like the Back Spin Out-to-In Axe Kick, the first half of the "spin back" motion can be likened to the "coiling" up of a high tension spring. While the second half of the "spin back" motion, as the ball of your base leg foot touches the ground after "spinning back" and stepping backward, releases the spring resulting in your body rapidly and explosively completing the "spin back" while simultaneously initiating the kick.

3/4 to Peak of Arc Front View *3/4 to Peak of Arc Side View*

Peak of Arc:

21. Your base leg foot should still be in approximately the same position, with your base leg knee being slightly bent. Your kicking leg has now moved up to the correct height to begin its downward trajectory.

22. The heel of the kicking foot should follow a straight line of trajectory from the "Peak of Arc" through the target (Impact), to the "Follow Through" position.

Peak of Arc
Foot Position

23. Your upper body should now be facing at a slight angle towards your opponent, while continuing to lean back slightly. In this position, the kicking leg side of your body will be closer to your opponent than your base leg side.

24. Although your body is in the above position, your back remains straight but not rigid, and your head should still be facing towards your opponent. Eye contact with your opponent is maintained at all times.

Note: The ability to effectively and efficiently utilize high section kicks depends primarily on the following four factors. A: Your expertise in kicking. B: Your overall flexibility and physical condition. C: Your environment at the time. D: Your opponent.

Peak of Arc Front View

Peak of Arc Side View

69

Impact:

25. Your entire base leg foot should now be in contact with the ground and gripping it, while in approximately the same position.

26. Your upper body, with the kicking leg side of your body remaining closer to your opponent than your base leg side, should still be facing at a slight angle towards your opponent, while continuing to lean back slightly. At the moment of impact, your entire body should tighten to add power to the kick, as your foot continues to travel on a downward trajectory through the target.

27. Notice how your kicking foot, kicking leg, hips, back, shoulders and head are all in alignment at the initial moment of "Impact." Also, notice how the toes of the kicking foot are pulled back towards your body and pointed up. This helps insure that contact with the target is made with the back of the heel.

28. Your head should still be facing towards your opponent. Eye contact with your opponent is maintained at all times.

Impact Foot Position

Note: Your kicking leg should be just as fast, if not faster, traveling from the "Peak of Arc" to the "Follow Through" position, than it is traveling from "Fighting Position" to the "Peak of Arc."

Impact Front View

Impact Side View

Follow Through:

29. Your entire base leg foot should remain in contact with the ground and gripping it, while in approximately the same position. The knee on your base leg will remain slightly bent.

30. Your upper body, with the kicking leg side of your body remaining closer to your opponent than your base leg side, should still be facing at a slight angle towards your opponent, while continuing to lean back slightly.

Follow Through Foot Position

31. Your kicking leg foot should continue along exactly the same downward path it followed from the "Peak of Arc" to "Impact." Your foot should now be at approximately knee level.

32. Your head should still be facing towards your opponent. Eye contact with your opponent is maintained at all times.

Note: Just like chopping a block of wood with an axe, if you do not use sufficient enough force when striking your opponent with an Axe Kick, your kick will not only be ineffective (perhaps causing minor damage to your opponent), but it may also become stuck on your opponent's shoulder, which would allow your opponent the opportunity to grab your leg.

Follow Through Front View   *Follow Through Side View*

71

Return to Fighting Position:
There are two ways that you can return to a fighting position from the "Follow Through" position. They are as follows:

33a. After you have reached the "Follow Through" position, simply bring your kicking foot behind you and set it down into a fighting position with your kicking leg behind you, rather than in front of you.

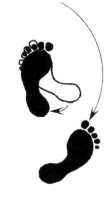

Position #1

33b. After you have reached the "Follow Through" position, simply leave your kicking foot in front of you and set it down into a fighting position with your kicking leg in front of you, rather than behind you.

Position #2

Note: Unlike the example illustrated for you on the previous page, a correctly executed Axe Kick should, as you can see in the illustration below, violently <u>EXPLODE</u> completely through your opponent like a lumberjack's axe chopping through a block of wood.

Pictorial Overview:

Fighting Position

Spin Back

Begin Arc

3/4 to Peak of Arc

Peak of Arc

Impact

Follow Through

Position #1

Position #2

Off-Setting Out-to-In Axe Kick

The Off-Setting Out-to-In Axe Kick is identical in execution to the Out-to-In Axe Kick, with one notable exception. A quick double step motion to the side (which puts you at a 45-degree angle from your original starting position), which is performed immediately prior to executing the kick. The starting position is the same as Out-to-In Axe Kick, in that your kicking foot is in the rear position. The actual double-step motion of the feet prior to the execution of the kick is performed by first moving the rearward foot and then the forward foot off at a 45-degree angle to the side of your opponent. When executing the double-step motion, be sure and move your rearward foot first, then your forward foot, without initially moving your hips and upper body in order to avoid telegraphing the move to your opponent. Your hips and upper body will begin to move when you begin to place the forward foot back onto the ground.

Fighting Position:

1. Your fighting position for this kick is exactly the same as it is for Out-to-In Axe Kick, in that your kicking leg will be in the rearward position.

2. This stance is approximately shoulder width apart with the heel of your rear foot directly in line with the heel of your front foot

3. Your front or lead foot should be pointed directly at your opponent.

4. Your rear foot is angled toward the right at approximately a 45-degree angle. Your weight should be distributed evenly over the balls of both feet.

5. Your knees are slightly, but not noticeably bent. They should not be locked straight or rigid.

Fighting Position
Foot Position

Fighting Position Front View

Fighting Position Side View

6. Your body should be facing at a 45-degree angle toward your opponent. This presents a smaller target area and also facilitates a faster off-set, which in turn allows you the opportunity to initiate a faster kick.

7. Your hands should be held up (like a boxer's), with the elbows tucked in to protect the ribs and your hands up to protect your head. Your hands should remain as close to this position as possible throughout the entire kick.

8. Your head should be facing your opponent with your chin tucked down and protected by your lead shoulder.

9. Your eyes should be centered on your opponent's chest.

Off-Set (part one):

10. Move your rear foot to the right (approximately 2-3 feet), and slightly forward (approximately 8 to 10 inches).

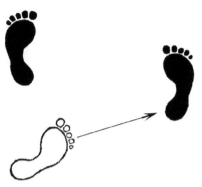

Off-Set Foot Position (part one)

First Step on Off-Set Front View

First Step on Off-Set Side View

Off-Set (part two):

11. Move your front foot to the right approximately 12 to 18 inches. Your body should now be in a Fighting Position at a 45 -degree angle from its original starting position.

Off-Set Foot Position (part two)

75

Begin Arc:

12. Using the toes of your kicking foot, push off the floor and bring your kicking leg up at approximately a 45-degree angle to your opponents left. Your leg should be straight, and your kicking foot should already be in the correct position to strike your opponent.

13. As your bring your kicking leg up, your upper body should start turning as it begins to face towards your opponent. Your back will remain

Begin Arc Foot Position

Second Step on Off-Set Front View

Second Step on Off-Set Side View

Begin Arc Front View

Begin Arc Side View

straight but not rigid.

14. Although your hands have switched position, they should still be held up (like a boxer's), with the elbows tucked in to protect the ribs and your hands up to protect your head.

15. Your head is up and facing towards your opponent, while your eyes remain in contact with your opponent throughout the entire kick.

3/4 to Peak of Arc:

16. Your base leg foot should now have moved approximately 45-degrees (counterclockwise) by pivoting on the ball of your foot, while the knee on your base leg remains slightly bent. Your kicking leg has now moved up to your opponent's head height, although still at a 45-degree angle to your opponents left.

17. Your kicking foot remains in the correct striking position throughout the entire sequence.

*3/4 to Peak of Arc
Foot Position*

18. Your upper body is now facing towards your opponent and leaning back slightly.

19. Although your body is in the above position, your back remains straight but not rigid, and your head should still be facing towards your opponent. Your eyes should continue to remain in contact with your opponent throughout the entire kick.

3/4 to Peak of Arc Front View   *3/4 to Peak of Arc Side View*

Peak of Arc:

20. Your base leg foot should still be in approximately the same position, with your base leg knee being slightly bent. Your kicking leg has now moved up to the correct height to begin its downward trajectory.

21. The heel of the kicking foot should follow a straight line of trajectory from the "Peak of Arc" through the target (Impact), to the "Follow Through" position.

22. Your upper body should now be facing at a slight angle towards your opponent, while continuing to lean back slightly. In this position, the kicking leg side of your body will be closer to your opponent than your base leg side.

23. Although your body is in the above position, your back remains straight but not rigid, and your head should still be facing towards your opponent. Eye contact with your opponent is maintained at all times.

Peak of Arc
Foot Position

Note: Due to the unique dynamics of an Axe Kick, your kicking foot will always have a slight pause at the peak of its upward "Path of Trajectory" just before beginning its descent along its downward "Path of Trajectory" to its target. Keeping this in mind as you look closely at these two photographs, see how vulnerable you are in this position. Constantly strive to kick faster than you can blink!

Peak of Arc Front View

Peak of Arc Side View

Impact:

24. Your entire base leg foot should now be in contact with the ground and gripping it, while in approximately the same position.

25. Your upper body, with the kicking leg side of your body remaining closer to your opponent than your base leg side, should still be facing at a slight angle towards your opponent, while continuing to lean back slightly. At the moment of impact, your entire body should tighten to add power to the kick, as your foot continues to travel on a downward trajectory through the target.

Impact Foot Position

26. Notice how your kicking foot, kicking leg, hips, back, shoulders and head are all in alignment at the initial moment of "Impact." Also, notice how the toes of the kicking foot are pulled back towards your body and pointed up. This helps insure that contact with the target is made with the back of the heel.

27. Your head should still be facing towards your opponent. Eye contact with your opponent is maintained at all times.

Note: After you have become sufficiently proficient executing the kicks described in this book wearing gi pants and being barefoot, you will want to also start practicing them wearing your normal everyday clothes and shoes. There is a big difference between kicking in gi pants and barefoot, and kicking in everyday clothes and shoes.

Impact Front View

Impact Side View

Follow Through:

28. Your entire base leg foot should remain in contact with the ground and gripping it, while in approximately the same position. The knee on your base leg will remain slightly bent.

29. Your upper body, with the kicking leg side of your body remaining closer to your opponent than your base leg side, should still be facing at a slight angle toward your opponent, while continuing to lean back slightly.

Follow Through Foot Position

30. Your kicking leg foot should continue along exactly the same downward path it followed from the "Peak of Arc" to "Impact." Your foot should now be at approximately knee level.

31. Your head should still be facing towards your opponent. Eye contact with your opponent is maintained at all times.

Note: Although this book details only one of the ten primary kicks and ten of its main variations. You must remember that there are nine more primary kicks, and many more variations of each of those kicks. Kicking is only one aspect of becoming a complete and effective fighter. One should also study and practice hand and elbow techniques, throwing, grappling, and joint techniques.

Follow Through Front View   *Follow Through Side View*

Return to Fighting Position:
There are two ways that you can return to a fighting position from the "Follow Through" position. They are as follows:

32a. After you have reached the "Follow Through" position, simply bring your kicking foot behind you and set it down into a fighting position with your kicking leg behind you, rather than in front of you.

Position #1

32b. After you have reached the "Follow Through" position, simply leave your kicking foot in front of you and set it down into a fighting position with your kicking leg in front of you, rather than behind you.

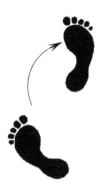

Position #2

Note: Both of these "Return to Fighting Position" positions, will be at a 45-degree angle to the right of your initial "Fighting Position."

Note: The "Off-Setting" movement is one of the primary techniques utilized in the "8 Directions of Attack" strategy. This is a very important strategic technique and one that can be utilized in any martial art.

Note: In order to generate the maximum amount of power possible when executing an Axe Kick, you must adhere to the correct execution of movement throughout the entire kicking sequence. Just as in boxing, power must first be generated by the movement of the feet, legs, hips, body, and shoulders, prior to <u>STRIKING THROUGH</u> your target.

81

Pictorial Overview:

Fighting Position   Off-Set (part one)   Off-Set (part two)

Begin Arc   3/4 to Peak of Arc   Peak of Arc

Impact   Follow Through

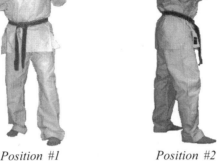

Position #1   *Position #2*

Note: As you look at the illustration below, imagine that your kicking foot and
kicking leg are represented by the head of the axe and the axe handle
respectively, while your opponent is represented by the block of wood. Do
you remember what I explained to you on page 14, about how if you apply
the correct striking implement to the correct vital/vulnerable point, it is
like chopping a block of wood with an axe. However, if you strike the
target incorrectly without applying all of the proper principles and correct techniques, your effectiveness will be greatly reduced and you may
cause more damage to yourself than you do your opponent. Proper utilization of your brain is very important in all aspects of life, not just the
martial arts, don't neglect it!

Switch Out-to-In Axe Kick

The Switch Out-to-In Axe Kick is identical in execution to the Out-to-In Axe Kick, with one notable exception. A switching motion of the feet, which is performed immediately prior to the execution of the kick. The switch is used to confuse the opponent and can also increase the power in this kick due to the added momentum of switching your feet. The starting position is the same as it is for Back Spin Out-to-In Axe Kick, with your kicking leg in the forward position rather than in the rearward position. The actual switching of the feet prior to execution of the kick is performed by simultaneously switching the position of both feet utilizing a straight line or scissors type motion. With the end result being a fighting position with the kicking leg now in the rearward position. When executing the switch, be sure and move your feet first without initially moving your hips and upper body in order to avoid telegraphing the switch to your opponent. Your hips and upper body will begin to move immediately after your feet, but not before.

Fighting Position:

1. Your fighting position for this kick is exactly the same as it was for Back Spin Out-to-In Axe Kick. With your kicking leg in the forward position to begin with rather than in the rearward position.

2. This stance is approximately shoulder width apart with the heel of your rear foot in a direct line with the heel of your front foot.

3. Your front or lead foot should be pointing directly at your opponent.

Fighting Position
Foot Position

Fighting Position Front View

Fighting Position Side View

84

4. Your rear foot is angled towards the left at approximately a 45-degree angle. Your weight should be distributed evenly over the balls of both feet.
5. Your knees are slightly, but not noticeably bent. They should not be locked or rigid.
6. Your body should be facing at a 45-degree angle toward your opponent. This presents a smaller target area and also facilitates a faster switch, which in turn allows you the opportunity to initiate a faster kick.
7. Your hands should be held up (like a boxer's), with the elbows tucked in to protect the ribs and your hands up to protect your head. Your hands should remain as close to this position as possible throughout the entire kick.
8. Your head should be facing your opponent with your chin tucked down and protected by your lead shoulder.
9. Your eyes should be centered on your opponents chest.

Switch Feet & Begin Arc:
10. Utilizing a scissors type motion of your legs and feet, simultaneously switch your front foot with your rear foot and vice versa. As soon as the ball of your front foot touches the ground in the rearward position, begin to execute the kick.
11. Using the toes of your kicking foot, push off the floor and bring your kicking leg up at approximately a 45-degree angle to your opponents left. Your leg should be straight, and your kicking foot should already be in the correct position to strike your opponent.

Switch Feet &
Begin Arc
Foot Position

Switch Feet & Begin Arc Front View   *Switch Feet & Begin Arc Side View*

85

12. As your bring your kicking leg up, your upper body should start turning as it begins to face towards your opponent. Your back will remain straight but not rigid.
13. Although your hands have switched position, they should still be held up (like a boxer's), with the elbows tucked in to protect the ribs and your hands up to protect your head.
14. Your head is up and facing towards your opponent, while your eyes remain in contact with your opponent throughout the entire kick.

3/4 to Peak of Arc:
15. Your base leg foot should now have moved approximately 45-degrees (counterclockwise) by pivoting on the ball of your foot, while the knee on your base leg remains slightly bent. Your kicking leg has now moved up to your opponent's head height, although still at a 45-degree angle to your opponents left.
16. Your kicking foot remains in the correct striking position throughout the entire sequence.
17. Your upper body is now facing towards your opponent and leaning back slightly.
18. Although your body is in the above position, your back remains straight but not rigid, and your head should still be facing towards your opponent. Your eyes should continue to remain in contact with your opponent throughout the entire kick.

*3/4 to Peak of Arc
Foot Position*

3/4 to Peak of Arc Front View   *3/4 to Peak of Arc Side View*

Peak of Arc:

19. Your base leg foot should still be in approximately the same position, with your base leg knee being slightly bent. Your kicking leg has now moved up to the correct height to begin its downward trajectory.

20. The heel of the kicking foot should follow a straight line of trajectory from the "Peak of Arc" through the target (Impact), to the "Follow Through" position.

21. Your upper body should now be facing at a slight angle towards your opponent, while continuing to lean back slightly. In this position, the kicking leg side of your body will be closer to your opponent than your base leg side.

22. Although your body is in the above position, your back remains straight but not rigid, and your head should still be facing towards your opponent. Eye contact with your opponent is maintained at all times.

Peak of Arc
Foot Position

Note: One of the most common, and often times comical, mistakes you can make when attempting to execute an Axe Kick is to raise your kicking leg up to the "Peak of Arc" position so fast and without maintaining strict control, that you actually knock your own base leg out from underneath you and you end up falling on your butt and/or back. That is one reason why you should always have a slight bend in your base leg knee as you bring your leg up to the "Peak of Arc" position.

Peak of Arc Front View

Peak of Arc Side View

Impact:

23. Your entire base leg foot should now be in contact with the ground and gripping it, while in approximately the same position.

24. Your upper body, with the kicking leg side of your body remaining closer to your opponent than your base leg side, should still be facing at a slight angle towards your opponent, while continuing to lean back slightly. At the moment of impact, your entire body should tighten to add power to the kick, as your foot continues to travel on a downward trajectory through the target.

Impact Foot Position

25. Notice how your kicking foot, kicking leg, hips, back, shoulders and head are all in alignment at the initial moment of "Impact." Also, notice how the toes of the kicking foot are pulled back towards your body and pointed up. This helps insure that contact with the target is made with the back of the heel.

26. Your head should still be facing towards your opponent. Eye contact with your opponent is maintained at all times.

Note: Your first line of defense should be your kicks, as they are your longest and most powerful weapons in your arsenal. Kicking falls into the "Long Range" category, while punching and hand strikes fall into the "Mid Range" category. Knee and elbow strikes fall into the "Short Range" category, while joint techniques fall into your final range, "Grappling."

Impact Front View   *Impact Side View*

Follow Through:

27. Your entire base leg foot should remain in contact with the ground and gripping it, while in approximately the same position. The knee on your base leg will remain slightly bent.

Follow Through Foot Position

28. Your upper body, with the kicking leg side of your body remaining closer to your opponent than your base leg side, should still be facing at a slight angle towards your opponent, while continuing to lean back slightly.

29. Your kicking leg foot should continue along exactly the same downward path it followed from the "Peak of Arc" to "Impact." Your foot should now be at approximately knee level.

30. Your head should still be facing towards your opponent. Eye contact with your opponent is maintained at all times.

Note: Due to the very nature and difficulty in effectively executing an Axe Kick on a standing, mentally focused opponent. I strongly recommend utilizing the Axe Kick as a finishing technique on a disoriented and preferably already injured opponent. As a general rule-of-thumb, just as a boxer sets up his opponent with several jabs before unloading on him with a straight cross or hook. You too should also set up your opponent with easier and faster techniques before dropping an Axe kick on him.

Follow Through Front View

Follow Through Side View

89

Return to Fighting Position:
There are two ways that you can return to a fighting position from the "Follow Through" position. They are as follows:

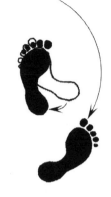 

31a. After you have reached the "Follow Through" position, simply bring your kicking foot behind you and set it down into a fighting position with your kicking leg behind you, rather than in front of you.

Position #1

31b. After you have reached the "Follow Through" position, simply leave your kicking foot in front of you and set it down into a fighting position with your kicking leg in front of you, rather than behind you.

Position #2

Note: One exercise that you can do to improve your foot switching skills (footwork), is to continuously switch your feet without kicking until given a prearranged signal by your training partner. As soon as you receive the signal, immediately kick with whichever foot you had just switched to the rearward position. Do this exercise for 10 minutes at a time with your training partner varying the length of time between signals. The time between signals can be anywhere from a second or two, to up to a minute. The idea here is not how many times you can kick, but how fast you can kick when an opportunity presents itself. This exercise along with countless others will be explained in greater detail in the forthcoming ten volume training series for improving your kicks.

Pictorial Overview:

Fighting Position

Switch Feet

Begin Arc

3/4 to Peak of Arc

Peak of Arc

Impact

Follow Through

Position #1

Position #2

Step Back Out-to-In Axe Kick

The Step Back Out-to-In Axe Kick is identical in execution to the Out-to-In Axe Kick, with one notable exception. A stepping backward motion, which is performed immediately prior to executing the kick. This stepping backward motion is used to either draw your opponent into you, or to avoid an attack. It can also increase the power in this kick due to the added momentum of stepping backward. The starting or fighting position for this kick begins with your kicking leg in the forward position rather than in the rear position. The actual stepping back motion of the forward foot prior to the execution of the kick, is performed by simply stepping back with the forward foot into another fighting position. Only now, the kicking leg is in the rearward rather than the forward position. When executing the stepping back motion, be sure and move your forward foot without initially moving your hips and upper body in order to avoid telegraphing the movement to your opponent. Your hips and upper body will begin to move as you set your foot back down on the ground.

Fighting Position:

1. Your fighting position for this kick is exactly the same as it was for Back Spin Out-to-In Axe Kick. With your kicking leg will be in the forward position to begin with rather than in the rearward position.
2. This stance is approximately shoulder width apart with the heel of your rear foot in a direct line with the heel of your front foot.
3. Your front or lead foot should be pointing directly at your opponent.

Fighting Position Foot Position

Fighting Position Front View

Fighting Position Side View

4. Your rear foot is angled towards the left at approximately a 45-degree angle. Your weight should be distributed evenly over the balls of both feet.
5. Your knees are slightly, but not noticeably bent. They should not be locked or rigid.
6. Your body should be facing at a 45-degree angle toward your opponent. This presents a smaller target area and also facilitates a faster step-back, which in turn allows you the opportunity to initiate a faster kick.
7. Your hands should be held up (like a boxer's), with the elbows tucked in to protect the ribs and your hands up to protect your head. Your hands should remain as close to this position as possible throughout the entire kick.
8. Your head should be facing your opponent with your chin tucked down and protected by your lead shoulder.
9. Your eyes should be centered on your opponents chest.

Step Back & Begin Arc:
10. Step back with your front foot approximately one shoulder width into another fighting position. As soon as the ball of your front foot touches the ground in the rearward position, begin to execute

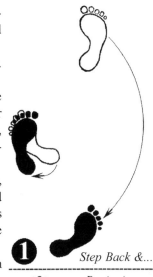
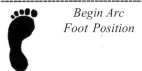

Step Back &...

*Begin Arc
Foot Position*

Step Back & Begin Arc Front View   *Step Back & Begin Arc Side View*

93

the kick.

11. Using the toes of your kicking foot, push off the floor and bring your kicking leg up at approximately a 45-degree angle to your opponents left. Your leg should be straight, and your kicking foot should already be in the correct position to strike your opponent.

12. As your bring your kicking leg up, your upper body should start turning as it begins to face towards your opponent. Your back will remain straight but not rigid.

13. Although your hands have switched position, they should still be held up (like a boxer's), with the elbows tucked in to protect the ribs and your hands up to protect your head.

14. Your head is up and facing towards your opponent, while your eyes remain in contact with your opponent throughout the entire kick.

3/4 to Peak of Arc:

15. Your base leg foot should now have moved approximately 45-degrees (counterclockwise) by pivoting on the ball of your foot, while the knee on your base leg remains slightly bent. Your kicking leg has now moved up to your opponent's head height, although still at a 45-degree angle to your opponents left.

16. Your kicking foot remains in the correct striking position throughout the entire sequence.

17. Your upper body is now facing towards your opponent and leaning back slightly.

*3/4 to Peak of Arc
Foot Position*

3/4 to Peak of Arc Front View   *3/4 to Peak of Arc Side View*

94

18. Although your body is in the above position, your back remains straight but not rigid, and your head should still be facing towards your opponent. Your eyes should continue to remain in contact with your opponent throughout the entire kick.

Peak of Arc:

19. Your base leg foot should still be in approximately the same position, with your base leg knee being slightly bent. Your kicking leg has now moved up to the correct height to begin its downward trajectory.

20. The heel of the kicking foot should follow a straight line of trajectory from the "Peak of Arc" through the target (Impact), to the "Follow Through" position.

Peak of Arc
Foot Position

21. Your upper body should now be facing at a slight angle towards your opponent, while continuing to lean back slightly. In this position, the kicking leg side of your body will be closer to your opponent than your base leg side.

22. Although your body is in the above position, your back remains straight but not rigid, and your head should still be facing towards your opponent. Eye contact with your opponent is maintained at all times.

Note: For optimum results upon impact, you must use a combination of proper technique, along with an explosive combination of speed and strength.

Peak of Arc Front View   *Peak of Arc Side View*

95

Impact:

23. Your entire base leg foot should now be in contact with the ground and gripping it, while in approximately the same position.

24. Your upper body, with the kicking leg side of your body remaining closer to your opponent than your base leg side, should still be facing at a slight angle towards your opponent, while continuing to lean back slightly. At the moment of impact, your entire body should tighten to add power to the kick, as your foot continues to travel on a downward trajectory through the target.

Impact Foot Position

25. Notice how your kicking foot, kicking leg, hips, back, shoulders and head are all in alignment at the initial moment of "Impact." Also, notice how the toes of the kicking foot are pulled back towards your body and pointed up. This helps insure that contact with the target is made with the back of the heel.

26. Your head should still be facing towards your opponent. Eye contact with your opponent is maintained at all times.

Note: Some schools/styles of martial arts teach their students to utilize the ball of the foot when executing an Axe Kick as this gives you another 4 to 6 inches of reach. While it is true that you can gain a few more inches of reach, it is not a very efficient way of doing so, and it also makes for a poor striking implement. Strike with the back of the heel, or not at all!

Impact Front View   *Impact Side View*

Follow Through:

27. Your entire base leg foot should remain in contact with the ground and gripping it, while in approximately the same position. The knee on your base leg will remain slightly bent.

28. Your upper body, with the kicking leg side of your body remaining closer to your opponent than your base leg side, should still be facing at a slight angle towards your opponent, while continuing to lean back slightly.

Follow Through Foot Position

29. Your kicking leg foot should continue along exactly the same downward path it followed from the "Peak of Arc" to "Impact." Your foot should now be at approximately knee level.

30. Your head should still be facing towards your opponent. Eye contact with your opponent is maintained at all times.

Note: One of the inherit dangers of executing an Axe Kick is the possibility of your kicking leg getting stuck up on top of your opponent's shoulder, or your opponent grabbing your kicking leg. Therefore, it is imperative that you practice retracting your leg from this precarious position by bringing your knee to your chest and then recoiling your kicking foot as if you had just executed a Front Kick.

Follow Through Front View   *Follow Through Side View*

Return to Fighting Position:
There are two ways that you can return to a fighting position from the "Follow Through" position. They are as follows:

31a. After you have reached the "Follow Through" position, simply bring your kicking foot behind you and set it down into a fighting position with your kicking leg behind you, rather than in front of you.

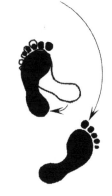

Position #1

31b. After you have reached the "Follow Through" position, simply leave your kicking foot in front of you and set it down into a fighting position with your kicking leg in front of you, rather than behind you.

Position #2

Note: If you have access to a basketball court or any similar area that is large and free of obstructions, you can try the following exercise to improve your footwork. Continuously step back alternating legs each time, until your training partner gives you a prearranged signal to kick. As soon as you receive the signal, immediately kick with whichever foot you had just switched to the rearward position. Once you reach the opposite end of the area you are working in, turn around and go back. Do this exercise for 10 minutes at a time with your training partner varying the number of steps between signals. The number of steps between signals can be anywhere from one or two, to several. The idea here is not how many times you can kick, but how fast you can kick when an opportunity presents itself. This exercise along with countless others will be explained in greater detail in the forthcoming ten volume training series for improving your kicks.

Pictorial Overview:

Fighting Position

Step Back

Begin Arc

3/4 to Peak of Arc

Peak of Arc

Impact

Follow Through

Position #1

Position #2

99

Back Spin Out-to-In Axe Kick
(With the left leg)

Here is an example on how to change the instructions presented in this book in order to execute the exact same kicks with the left leg. First of all you're going to be kicking with the left leg rather than the right, so your rear foot and body position will be exactly opposite of those that you would use if you were kicking with the right leg. To put it simply, kicking with the left leg should mirror exactly those kicks performed with the right leg and vice versa.

Fighting Position:

1. Your fighting position for this kick is the exact same as for Out-to-In Axe Kick. However, since you are going to be kicking with the left leg, it will be in the forward position to begin with rather than in the rearward position.

2. This stance is approximately shoulder width apart with the heel of your rear foot in a direct line with the heel of your front foot.

3. Your front or lead foot should be pointing directly at your opponent.

4. Your rear foot is angled towards the right at approximately a 45-degree angle. Your weight should be distributed evenly over the balls of both feet.

5. Your knees are slightly, but not noticeably bent. They should not be locked straight or rigid.

6. Your body should be facing at a 45-degree angle toward

Fighting Position
Foot Position

Fighting Position Front View

Fighting Position Side View

100

your opponent. This presents a smaller target area and also facilitates a faster back-spin forward and-turn, which allows you the opportunity to initiate a faster kick.

7. Your hands should be held up (like a boxer's), with the elbows tucked in to protect the ribs and your hands up to protect your head. Your hands should remain as close to this position as possible throughout the entire kick.

8. Your head should be facing your opponent with your chin tucked down and protected by your lead shoulder.

9. Your eyes should be centered on your opponent's chest.

Back Spin & Step Forward:

10. Pivoting on the ball of your lead leg foot, turn clockwise and step forward with your rear foot approximately your shoulder width into another fighting position. As you are moving your rear foot forward, be sure and keep your weight centered over your lead leg. Also, don't make a big sweeping motion with your rear foot as you move it forward, keep it in close to your base leg foot as you turn. This helps maintain your balance while giving you a direct line of trajectory to your target.

11. As you execute the back spin, your back will

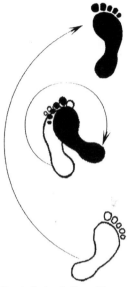

*Back Spin & Step Forward
Foot Position*

Back Spin & Step Forward Front View   *Back Spin & Step Forward Side View*

momentarily be facing directly toward your opponent at approximately the midway point in the back spin. As you are completing the back spin, you will begin to execute the kick.

12. While you are back-spinning forward, you should be turning your head and looking over your (non-kicking) leg shoulder. This will enable you to maintain eye contact with your opponent throughout the entire movement.

Turn & Begin Arc:

13. When the ball of your base leg foot touches the ground, utilize the toes of your kicking foot and push off the floor bringing your kicking leg up at approximately a 45-degree angle to your opponents right. Your leg should be straight, and your kicking foot should already be in the correct position to strike your opponent.

14. As your bring your kicking leg up, your upper body should start turning as it begins to face towards your opponent. Your back will remain straight but not rigid.

15. Although your hands have switched position, they should still be held up (like a boxer's), with the elbows tucked in to protect the ribs and your hands up to protect your head.

Begin Arc Foot Position

16. Your head is up and facing towards your opponent, while your eyes remain in contact with your opponent throughout the entire kick.

Note: Utilize deception when fighting. Make your opponent believe that you are going to do one thing, when you really intend to do another.

Turn & Begin Arc Front View   *Turn & Begin Arc Side View*

3/4 to Peak of Arc:

17. Your base leg foot should now have moved approximately 45-degrees (clockwise) by pivoting on the ball of your foot, while the knee on your base leg remains slightly bent. Your kicking leg has now moved up to your opponent's head height, although still at a 45-degree angle to your opponents right.

3/4 to Peak of Arc Foot Position

18. Your kicking foot remains in the correct striking position throughout the entire sequence.
19. Your upper body is now facing towards your opponent and leaning back slightly.
20. Although your body is in the above position, your back remains straight but not rigid, and your head should still be facing towards your opponent. Your eyes should continue to remain in contact with your opponent throughout the entire kick.

Note: The principles and techniques described within this book are not specific to any particular style. The information supplied within this book is intended to be used by any martial artist, practicing any style, anywhere in the world.

3/4 to Peak of Arc Front View   *3/4 to Peak of Arc Side View*

Peak of Arc:

21. Your base leg foot should still be in approximately the same position, with your base leg knee being slightly bent. Your kicking leg has now moved up to the correct height to begin its downward trajectory.

22. The heel of the kicking foot should follow a straight line of trajectory from the "Peak of Arc" through the target (Impact), to the "Follow Through" position.

Peak of Arc
Foot Position

23. Your upper body should now be facing at a slight angle towards your opponent, while continuing to lean back slightly. In this position, the kicking leg side of your body will be closer to your opponent than your base leg side.

24. Although your body is in the above position, your back remains straight but not rigid, and your head should still be facing towards your opponent. Eye contact with your opponent is maintained at all times.

Note: As a general rule-of-thumb, your initial impact point is at the surface of the target area (Vital/Vulnerable Point) in which you intend to STRIKE THROUGH. Your impact continues THROUGH the body or head, and ends outside of the body on the opposite side. Remember, DO NOT PUSH your opponent, STRIKE THROUGH your opponent.

Peak of Arc Front View

Peak of Arc Side View

Impact:

25. Your entire base leg foot should now be in contact with the ground and gripping it, while in approximately the same position.

26. Your upper body, with the kicking leg side of your body remaining closer to your opponent than your base leg side, should still be facing at a slight angle towards your opponent, while continuing to lean back slightly. At the moment of impact, your entire body should tighten to add power to the kick, as your foot continues to travel on a downward trajectory through the target.

27. Notice how your kicking foot, kicking leg, hips, back, shoulders and head are all in alignment at the initial moment of "Impact." Also, notice how the toes of the kicking foot are pulled back towards your body and pointed up. This helps insure that contact with the target is made with the back of the heel.

28. Your head should still be facing towards your opponent. Eye contact with your opponent is maintained at all times.

*Impact
Foot Position*

Note: The key to success in any endeavor you wish to pursue is this, self-discipline. Ask yourself this questions, "Are you willing to do whatever you have to, in order to get what you want?"

Impact Front View

Impact Side View

105

Follow Through:

29. Your entire base leg foot should remain in contact with the ground and gripping it, while in approximately the same position. The knee on your base leg will remain slightly bent.

Follow Through Foot Position

30. Your upper body, with the kicking leg side of your body remaining closer to your opponent than your base leg side, should still be facing at a slight angle towards your opponent, while continuing to lean back slightly.

31. Your kicking leg foot should continue along exactly the same downward path it followed from the "Peak of Arc" to "Impact." Your foot should now be at approximately knee level.

32. Your head should still be facing towards your opponent. Eye contact with your opponent is maintained at all times.

Note: At the end of your workout, execute an Axe Kick as slow as you can, while maintaining strict form and control. Pay close attention to how each body part feels while executing each individual phase of the kick.

Follow Through Front View   *Follow Through Side View*

Return to Fighting Position:
There are two ways that you can return to a fighting position from the "Follow Through" position. They are as follows:

Position #1

33a. After you have reached the "Follow Through" position, simply leave your kicking foot in front of you and set it down into a fighting position with your kicking leg in front of you, rather than behind you.

33b. After you have reached the "Follow Through" position, simply bring your kicking foot behind you and set it down into a fighting position with your kicking leg behind you, rather than in front of you.

Position #2

Note: If you are like the vast majority of martial artists, you will have one leg that is very good at kicking and the other that seems to lag behind. One thing that I do to correct this, is to perform 15 repetitions on my weak leg for every 10 repetitions that I perform with my strong leg. This works well for me and is a training technique you may want to try yourself.

Note: Although a separate ten volume set of books focusing on the combat and tournament applications of each of the ten primary kicks is currently being written, I would like to have you consider the following, "Couldn't the very motion of the "back spin" also be a Turning Back Kick followed by an Out-to-In Axe Kick?"

107

Pictorial Overview:

Fighting Position

Back Spin

Turn & Begin Arc

3/4 to Peak of Arc

Peak of Arc

Impact

Follow Through

Position #1

Position #2

Note: The In-to-Out Axe Kick is executed almost identically to the Out-to-In Axe Kick with one small difference. Instead of initiating the kick by bringing your leg up from the outside of your body to the "Peak of Arc," you initiate the In-to-Out Axe Kick by bringing your leg up and across the front of your body to the "Peak of Arc." As you look at the illustration below, you can see that I swing the axe up (1) and across the front of my body (2) in a clockwise (counterclockwise from your perspective) motion until the axe reaches its "Peak of Arc" (3), which is when I change direction and bring the axe straight down in front of me and through the block of wood (4).

In-to-Out Axe Kick

The Axe Kick is one of the ten primary kicks associated with Karate and/or Tae Kwon Do. Although it goes by many different names, the Axe Kick, when performed properly, is one of the most powerful kicks in the martial artist's arsenal. This section will go into minute detail over all areas and phases of the In-to-Out Axe Kick. Once this co-primary kick is mastered, all of the other variations of this co-primary kick will fall into place. Without any further ado, let's get started.

Fighting Stance:

Your fighting stance should be approximately shoulder width apart (1a) with the toes of your front or lead foot pointed directly at your opponent. The heel of your lead foot should be in a direct line (1b) with the heel of your rear foot. This allows you the opportunity to initiate a faster kick. Remember that the foot positions in this stance will actually change after you become comfortable executing this kick. At that time your feet will still be approximately shoulder width apart in length, however the heels will be about 4 to 8 inches apart, rather than in a straight line with one another.

The toes of your back or rear foot (1b) should be pointed away from your body at a 45-degree angle. For example, if your right foot were in the rear position, then the toes of that foot would be pointed to the right at a 45-degree angle. If the left foot were in the rear position, then the toes of your left foot would be pointed to the left at a 45-degree angle.

Your weight should be distributed over the balls of both feet and not over the entire surface are of the feet. This way your mobility is increased and you will be able to facilitate a faster turn when executing the kick. The weight distribution over your feet should be approximately 55% over the lead leg and 45% over the rear leg. This also allows for faster movement when kicking or when evading your opponent's attack.

Your knees (2) should be slightly but not noticeably bent. The lead leg knee should be slightly bent over the lead leg foot in the direction of the toes. The same also holds true for the rear knee in the fact that it too should be slightly bent over the rear foot in the direction of the rear toes. The bending of the knees contributes to faster movement with the legs as they are not locked straight or rigid and have better mobility when slightly bent rather than straight.

Your body (3) is facing at a 45-degree angle to your opponent. This presents a smaller target area facing toward your opponent. It also allows you better mobility moving forward toward your opponent, or backward away from your opponent. Additionally it allows you quicker access to off-set your opponent by moving in the direction your body is facing.

Your hands (4a) and elbows (4b), should be held up like a boxer's, that is with the lead hand held up at head level and away from your face about 8 to 12 inches (toward your opponent). Your lead elbow should be tucked in along your side in order to protect your ribs and stomach area. Your rear hand is held up alongside your cheek or neck, with the palm of that hand facing toward your cheek. Your rear

110

elbow is also tucked in along your side in order to protect your ribs and stomach area.

Your back (5) should be straight but not rigid and your lead shoulder should be raised up slightly in order to protect your chin.

Your head (6) is facing toward your opponent with the chin tucked down behind your upraised lead shoulder.

Your eyes (7) should focus like a flashlight on your opponent's chest to center your vision. At the same time, allow your peripheral vision to scan the rest of your opponent's body and therefore any movements he will make. A word of caution, <u>**do not**</u> become fixated on a particular spot or point of focus on your opponent. This becomes more of a hindrance than an asset when fighting.

Additionally, you should **never** take your eyes off your opponent for any reason. This mistake is quite common when first learning how to kick. A lot of students tend to watch their foot as it travels from the floor to its intended target. This is not only incorrect, but it can be very dangerous! Always maintain proper eye contact with your opponent. Remember the old saying, "Look before you leap?"

Fighting Position Foot Position (Beginning)

Fighting Position Foot Position (Advanced)

Note: To better understand the visual aspects of an In-to-Out Axe Kick, imagine that you have a "front view" and that you are looking at yourself standing in front of the protractor image which is shown on the right. In a "Fighting Position," your base leg (0), which in this case is your left leg, is at the 0-degree position, while your kicking leg (1), in this case the right leg, is at approximately the (negative) 15-degree position.

Front View

111

Fighting Position Front View

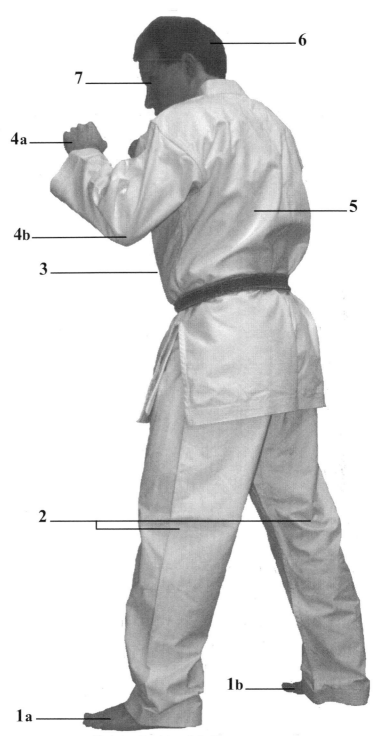

Fighting Position Side View

113

Begin Arc:

Shifting your weight onto your base leg foot (8), while simultaneously pivoting 45-degrees counterclockwise on the ball of your base leg foot, push off the floor utilizing the toes of your kicking foot (11), and bring your kicking leg up and across the front of your body at approximately a 45-degree angle to your left (your opponents right), while keeping your kicking leg and knee (10) straight, but not locked. This will place 100% of your weight onto your base leg, while your base leg knee (9) remains slightly bent. As soon as your kicking foot leaves the ground, it should already be in the correct position to strike your opponent.

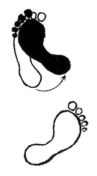

Begin Arc
Foot Position

As your kicking leg begins its upward "Path of Trajectory," your upper body (12a) should have turned 90-degrees counterclockwise (if kicking with the right leg, clockwise if you are kicking with the left leg), and is now facing at approximately a 45-degree angle to your left (your opponents right). In this position, your kicking leg side of your body will be closer to your opponent than your base leg side. Be sure and keep your back (12b) as straight as possible, but not rigid.

Your hands (13a) and elbows (13b) should still be in relatively the same position as they were in fighting position. That is like a boxer's with the lead hand held up at head level and away from your face about 8 to 12 inches (toward your opponent). Your lead elbow should be tucked in along your side in order to protect your ribs and stomach area. Your rear hand is held up alongside your cheek or neck, with the palm of that hand facing toward your cheek. Your rear elbow is also tucked in along your side in order to protect your ribs and stomach area.

Your back (12b) should be straight and facing away from your opponent. You should not be hunched over or bent forward at the waist. However, you should be leaning slightly back.

Your head (14) is facing straight ahead, and focused on your opponent's chest like a flashlight, not a laser beam. Your chin is tucked down behind your kicking leg shoulder, and your eyes (15) should still be centered on your opponent's chest.

Note: Maintaining the same visual perspective as you had in the previous illustration on page 111, and in the following illustrations on pages 117 and 120, imagine that you are beginning to execute the In-to-Out Axe Kick. Begin by raising your kicking leg from the "Fighting Position" (1) at approximately the (negative) 15-degree position, to the "Begin Arc" position (2), which is located at approximately the 70-degree position. While your base leg (0) remains at the 0-degree position.

Front View

114

Upward Path of Trajectory

14
15
13a
12b
13b
12a
10
11
9
8

Begin Arc Front View

115

Begin Arc Side View

3/4 to Peak of Arc:

As your kicking leg and foot continue along their upward "Path of Trajectory," your base foot (16) which now bears 100% of your weight after shifting the weight onto it in order to begin execution of the kick, should still be in approximately the same position.

3/4 to Peak of Arc Foot Position

The base leg knee (17) remains slightly bent in the direction of the toes of the base foot. Your kicking leg and foot (19) has now moved up to your opponent's head height by continuing along the upward "Path of Trajectory," while maintaining approximately a 45-degree angle to your left (your opponents right). Your toes should be flexed towards your kicking leg knee, so that with your leg extended, your heel will strike the target rather than your toes or sole of your foot. Your kicking leg and knee (18) should remain straight, but not locked. Once your kicking foot (19) has left the ground, it should remain in the correct striking position throughout the entire kick until returning back to the ground. After your foot has left the ground, the muscles in your thigh contract to bring your leg up into the "Peak of Arc" position.

Your upper body (20a) should still remain at a slight angle toward your opponent, with the kicking leg side of your body closer to your opponent than your base leg side. Your back (20b) should remain straight, but not rigid, throughout the entire kick. However, it should continue to lean slightly back.

Too many martial artists are sacrificing a proper upward "Path of Trajectory" in order to get the kick to the "Peak of Arc" and therefore, to the target faster. Although it is true to a certain extent that a kick will get to the "Peak of Arc" and therefore, to the target faster without utilizing the correct upward "Path of Trajectory," it is incorrect and can prove potentially harmful to the individual kicker. Proper technique should never be sacrificed for the sake of speed.

Your hands (21a) and elbows (21b), are also in relatively the same position as in (13a) and (13b), although they will occasionally change position to coincide with the various changes in body position, which take place throughout the execution of this kick. Your head (22) remains in the same position as in (14). Your eyes (23) are still focused on your opponent's chest like a flashlight, not a laser beam.

Note: As your kicking leg continues along its upward "Path of Trajectory," it will have moved from the "Begin Arc" position (2), to the "3/4 to Peak of Arc" position (3), which is located at approximately the 140-degree position. Although you will be pivoting on the ball of your base leg foot, your base leg (0) should remain at the 0-degree position.

Front View

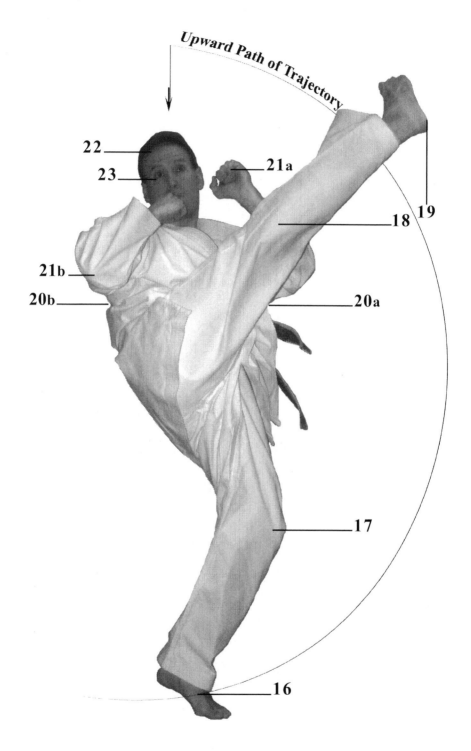

Upward Path of Trajectory

22

23

21a

21b

20b

20a

18 19

17

16

3/4 to Peak of Arc Front View

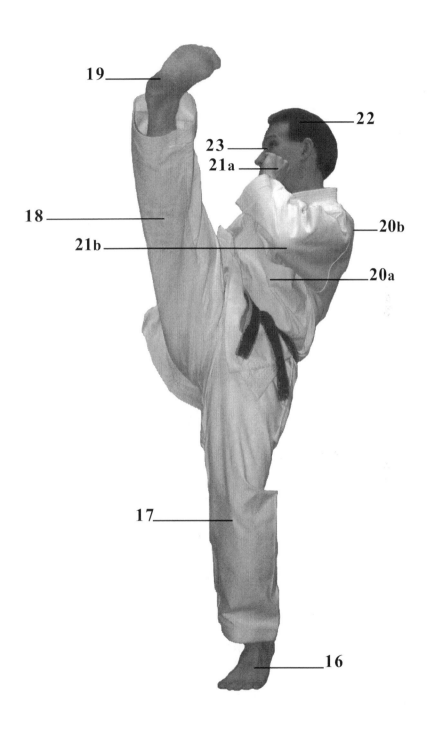

3/4 to Peak of Arc Side View

Peak of Arc:

Your base foot (24) remains in approximately the same position as in (16). Your base leg knee (25) is still slightly bent as you reach the "Peak of Arc." Your kicking leg and knee remain straight (but not locked), as they have now moved up to the correct height and position in order to begin their downward "Path of Trajectory." In this position, your kicking leg from your hip all the way up to your kicking leg heel (27), should be in a straight vertical line and flush against your upper torso and chest (28a). The toes of your kicking foot (27) are pointed directly behind you and flexed back toward your knee in order to fully expose the heel of your kicking foot as the striking implement. Although your toes and foot are flexed towards the kicking leg knee, do not flex them to the point of having your foot and ankle too tight. It should be a relaxed tension or flexion.

*Peak of Arc
Foot Position*

When looking at the downward "Path of Trajectory" from the front view, the heel of your kicking foot (27) will follow a straight line of trajectory from the "Peak of Arc" through the target (Impact) and continuing through to the "Follow Through" position. However, when you look at the downward "Path of Trajectory" from the side view, the heel of your kicking foot appears to be traveling in a crescent type motion. This is correct.

Your upper body (28a) should remain facing at a slight angle towards your opponent, with the kicking leg side of your body closer to your opponent than your base leg side. Your back (28b) remains straight but not rigid, and is facing away from your opponent, while continuing to lean back slightly.

Your hands (29a), and elbows (29b), are still in relatively the same position as previously described during the initial "Fighting Position." That is like a boxer's, with your hands up high around your chest and chin, and your elbows along side your rib cage.

Your head (30) remains facing directly toward your opponent with your chin tucked down into your chest. Your eyes (31) should be looking straight ahead, and focused on your opponent's chest.

Note: Your kicking leg will have continued its upward "Path of Trajectory" and has now moved the remaining 40-degrees from the "3/4 to Peak of Arc" position (3), to the "Peak of Arc" position (4), which is located at the 180-degree position. Although you will be pivoting on the ball of your base leg foot, your base leg (0) should remain at the 0-degree position.

Note: During the downward "Path of Trajectory," your kicking foot will travel in a straight line from the "Peak of Arc" (4) all the way down to the "Follow Through" position (0).

Front View

120

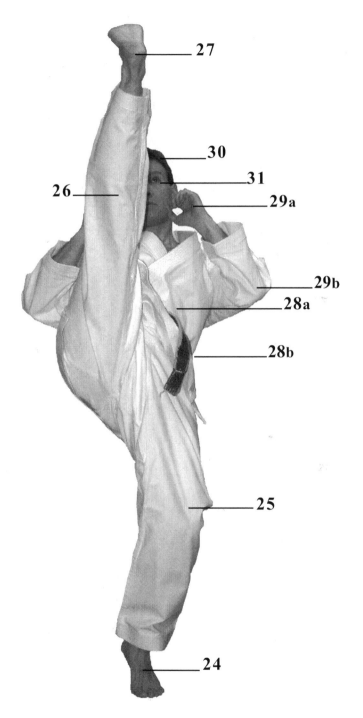

27

30

31

26

29a

29b

28a

28b

25

24

Peak of Arc Front View

121

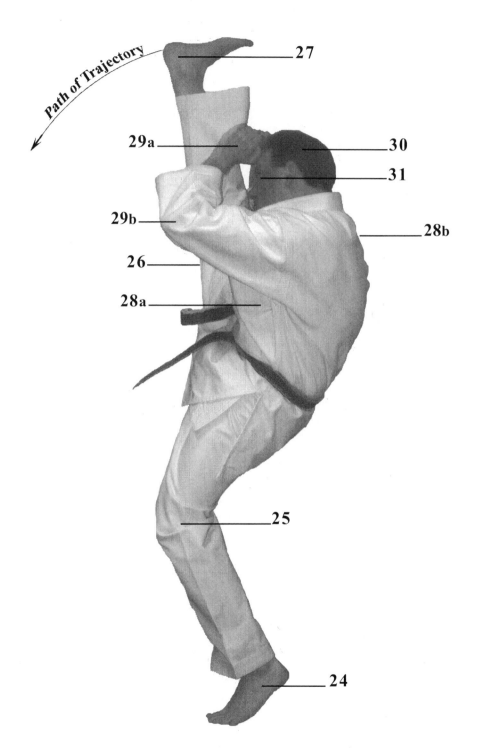

Path of Trajectory

27

29a

30

31

29b

28b

26

28a

25

24

Peak of Arc Side View

Impact:

Your entire base leg foot (32) should now be in contact with the ground, while simultaneously gripping the floor with the entire foot. In other words, your entire foot should be in solid contact with the ground with the toes still pointed at a 45-degree angle to your left (your opponents right). Your base leg knee (33) is now straightened slightly, but not locked, at the moment of impact to add power to the kick.

Impact
Foot Position

The heel of your kicking foot (35), with the toes pulled back and towards your kicking knee, should now be making contact with the appropriate, vital or vulnerable point, in one of the selected target areas on your opponent. Remember that the contact time between your striking implement and the opponent's target area is minimal. Do not push the technique to the target area and then let it hang in the air. Explosively strike through the target and get your foot back down on the ground!

At the moment of impact, your entire kicking leg from the heel (35) to the hips, along with your back (36b), shoulders, and head (38), should be in alignment while the entire body tightens immediately upon impact with the target, and then relaxes again, in order to facilitate a faster follow through. In order to help prevent injury, at the moment of impact, there should be a slight bend in your kicking leg knee (34).

Your upper body (36a), should still be facing at a slight angle towards your opponent, with the kicking leg side of your body closer to your opponent than your base leg side. Your back (36b) remains straight but not rigid, and is facing away from your opponent, while continuing to lean back slightly.

Your hands (37a) and elbows (37b), should still be up in relatively the same position as before in (29a) and (29b). Do not let them fly all over like a bird flapping its wings. Keep the elbows in to protect the rib cage and your hands up to protect your head.

Your head (38) is still facing towards your opponent with the chin tucked down into your chest. Your eyes (39) should still be looking straight ahead, and focused on your opponent's chest.

Note: To better understand the visual aspects of an In-to-Out Axe Kick from the "Peak of Arc" position to the "Return to Fighting Position," imagine that you have a "side view" and that you are looking at yourself standing in front of the protractor image which is shown on the right. Your kicking leg, which has completed its upward "Path of Trajectory," will now travel along its downward "Path of Trajectory" from the "Peak of Arc" position (5) approximately 40-degrees where it will make initial contact with your opponent at the "Impact" position (6). Your base leg (0) should remain at the 0-degree position.

Side View

123

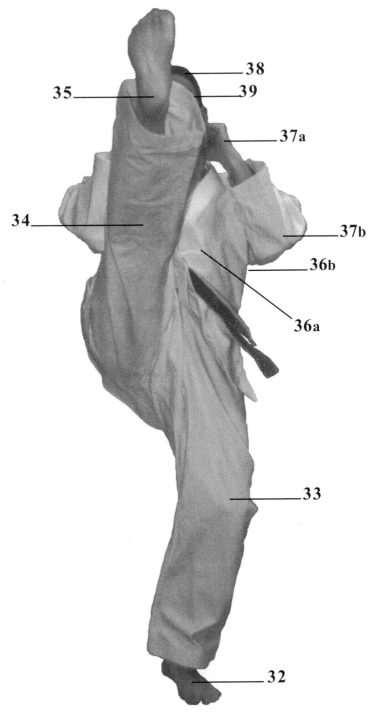

35

38

39

37a

34

37b

36b

36a

33

32

Impact Front View

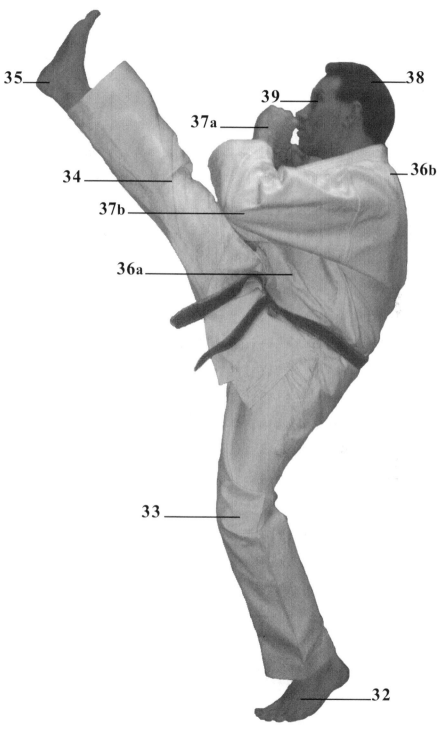

Impact Side View

125

Follow Through:

Your entire base leg foot (40) should remain in contact with the ground, while simultaneously gripping the floor with the entire foot. In other words, your entire foot should be in solid contact with the ground with the toes still pointed at a 45-degree angle to your left (your opponents right). Your base leg knee (41) although straight, should have a slight bend in it. The kicking leg knee (42) remains straight, but not locked. While your kicking foot (43), which should have continued along the same downward "Path of Trajectory" from the "Peak of Arc" to "Impact," should be straight in front of you at approximately the height of your base leg knee (41). The toes on your kicking foot (43) should remain flexed back towards your kicking leg knee. Although they will begin to relax as they move from this position back down to the ground.

Follow Through Foot Position

Too many martial artists seem to have a tendency to leave their kicks "hanging" in the air after executing a kick, rather than completing their kicks and returning them back down to the ground. My instructors used to call this "posing your kicks." This is an **extremely bad habit** to get into and one that needs to be corrected immediately.

Always remember, that your kicking foot should travel from the target back to its original starting position just as fast, if not faster, than it did from its initial fighting position to the target.

Your upper body (44a) should still be facing at a slight angle towards your opponent, with the kicking leg side of your body closer to your opponent than your base leg side. Your back (44b) remains straight but not rigid, and is facing away from your opponent, while continuing to lean back slightly.

Your hands (45a) and elbows (45b), are also in relatively the same position as they were in (37a) and (37b).

Your head (46) remains in relatively the same position that it has been in throughout the entire kick. Your eyes (47), if you executed the kick properly, should be still be on your opponent, although they may not be focused on your opponent's chest if you have knocked him down. **Never take your eyes off of your opponent.**

Note: Maintaining the same visual perspective as you had in the previous illustration on page 123, and in the following illustrations on page 133, imagine that you have just made initial contact with your opponent at the "Impact" point (6), and have continued to strike through your opponent. Your kicking foot will continue to travel along its downward "Path of Trajectory" approximately 70-degrees to the "Follow Through" position (7). While your base leg (0) continues to remain at the 0-degree position.

Side View

126

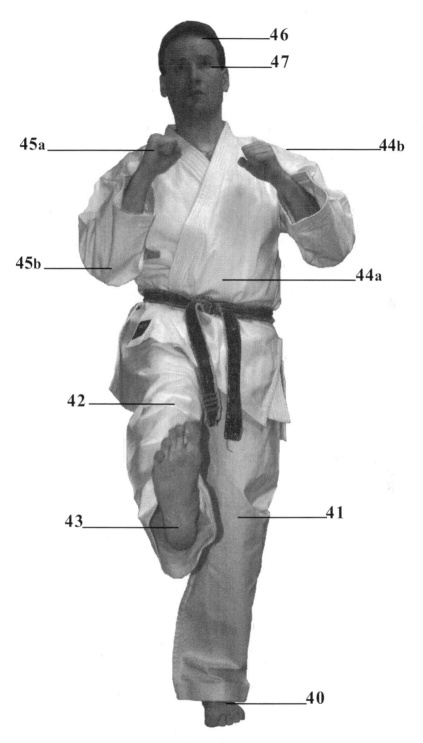

46
47
45a
44b
45b
44a
42
41
43
40

Follow Through Front View

127

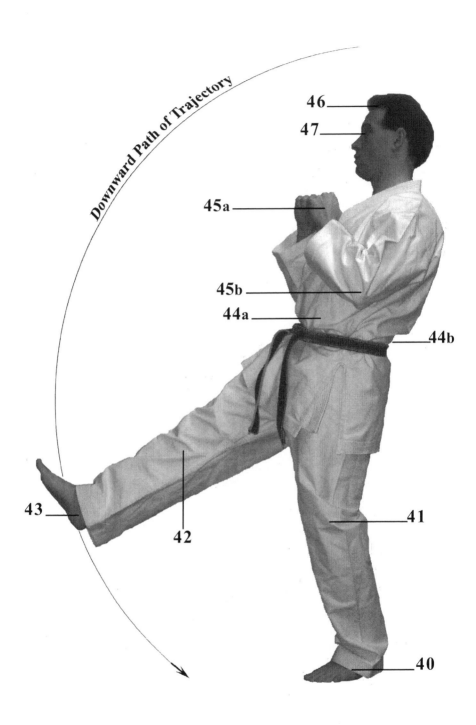

Follow Through Side View

Return to Fighting Position #1:

After you have reached the "Follow Through" position, pivot 45-degrees clockwise (if kicking with the right leg, counterclockwise if you are kicking with the left leg) by pivoting on the ball of your base leg foot, and returning your kicking foot back to its original starting position. Your head, shoulders and hips will all come back around to your original fighting position before your kicking leg foot touches the ground. Your entire body should be upright and straight although not rigid throughout the entire return to your original fighting position.

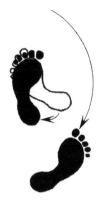

Position #1

Once you return to Fighting Position, your fighting stance should once again be approximately shoulder width apart (48a) with the toes of your front or lead foot pointed directly at your opponent. The heel of your lead foot should be in a direct line (48b) with the heel of your rear foot. The toes of your back or rear foot (48b) should be pointed away from your body at a 45-degree angle. For example, if your right foot were in the rear position, then the toes of that foot would be pointed to the right at a 45-degree angle. If the left foot were in the rear position, then the toes of your left foot would be pointed to the left at a 45-degree angle.

Your weight should once again be distributed over the balls of both feet and not over the entire surface are of the feet. The weight distribution over your feet should be approximately 55% over the lead leg and 45% over the rear leg.

Your knees (49) should be slightly but not noticeably bent. The lead leg knee should be slightly bent over the lead leg foot in the direction of the toes. The same also holds true for the rear knee in the fact that it too should be slightly bent over the rear foot in the direction of the rear toes. The bending of the knees contributes to faster movement with the legs as they are not locked straight or rigid and have better mobility when slightly bent rather than straight.

Your body (50) is facing at a 45-degree angle to your opponent. Your hands (51a) and elbows (51b), should still be held up like a boxer's, that is with the lead hand held up at head level and away from your face about 8 to 12 inches (toward your opponent). Your lead elbow should be tucked in along your side in order to protect your ribs and stomach area. Your rear hand is held up alongside your cheek with the palm of that hand facing toward your cheek. Your rear elbow is also tucked in along your side in order to protect your ribs and stomach area.

Your back (52) should be straight but not rigid and your lead shoulder should be raised up slightly in order to protect your chin.

Your head (53) is facing toward your opponent with the chin tucked down behind your upraised lead shoulder. Your eyes (54) should focus like a flashlight on the chest or center of your opponent whether he is still standing or not. At the same time, allow your peripheral vision to scan the rest of your opponent's body and therefore any movements he will make. I cannot stress this enough, **do not** become fixated on a particular spot or point of focus on your opponent. This becomes more of a hindrance than an asset when fighting.

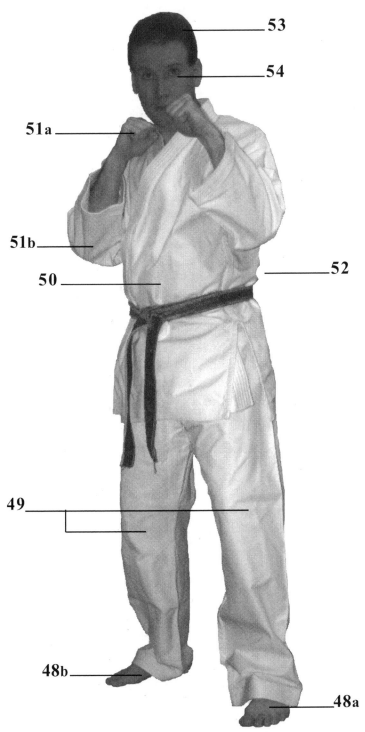

Return to Fighting Position #1 Front View

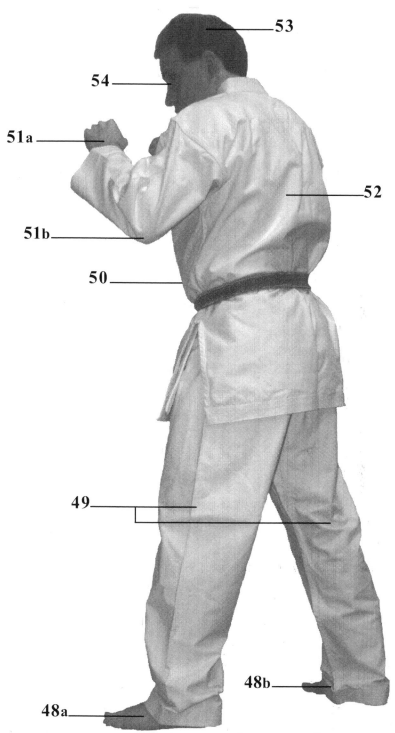

Return to Fighting Position #1 Side View

Return to Fighting Position #2:

After you have reached the "Follow Through" position, simply set your kicking foot down in front of you and toward your opponent, with your kicking leg in the forward position rather than in the rearward position. Your head, shoulders and hips will all move into another fighting position before your kicking leg foot touches the ground in front of you.

Your entire body should be upright and straight although not rigid throughout the entire return to your new fighting position. Remember that by stepping forward after this kick, you may be putting yourself in a more dangerous position because you are stepping in toward your opponent, which will put you closer to him. Be extra cautious when executing this move.

Position #2

Once you return to a Fighting Position, your fighting stance should once again be approximately shoulder width apart (55a) with the toes of your front or lead foot pointed directly at your opponent. The heel of your lead foot should be in a direct line (55b) with the heel of your rear foot. The toes of your back or rear foot (55b) should be pointed away from your body at a 45-degree angle. For example, if your left foot were in the rear position, then the toes of that foot would be pointed to the left at a 45-degree angle. If the right foot were in the rear position, then the toes of your right foot would be pointed to the right at a 45-degree angle.

Your weight should once again be distributed over the balls of both feet and not over the entire surface are of the feet. The weight distribution over your feet should be approximately 55% over the lead leg and 45% over the rear leg.

Your knees (56) should be slightly but not noticeably bent. The lead leg knee should be slightly bent over the lead leg foot in the direction of the toes. The same also holds true for the rear knee in the fact that it too should be slightly bent over the rear foot in the direction of the rear toes. The bending of the knees contributes to faster movement with the legs as they are not locked straight or rigid and have better mobility when slightly bent rather than straight.

Your body (57) is facing at a 45-degree angle to your opponent. Your hands (58a) and elbows (58b), should still be held up like a boxer's, that is with the lead hand held up at head level and away from your face about 8 to 12 inches (toward your opponent). Your lead elbow should be tucked in along your side in order to protect your ribs and stomach area. Your rear hand is held up alongside your cheek with the palm of that hand facing toward your cheek. Your rear elbow is also tucked in along your side in order to protect your ribs and stomach area.

Your back (59) should be straight but not rigid and your lead shoulder should be raised up slightly in order to protect your chin.

Your head (60) is facing toward your opponent with the chin tucked down behind your upraised lead shoulder. Your eyes (61) should focus like a flashlight on the chest or center of your opponent whether he is still standing or not. At the same time, allow your peripheral vision to scan the rest of your opponent's body and therefore any movements he will make.

132

Note: Just as I previously explained to you on page 49, if you paid close attention to the photographs from the "3/4 to Peak of Arc" position to "Impact," you will see that, once again, I have intentionally demonstrated one of the most common mistakes that is made when executing either an Out-to-In Axe Kick or an In-to-Out Axe Kick. That is executing the kick while balancing on the ball of your base leg foot. This is incorrect! Your entire base leg foot should always remain in total contact with the ground at the moment of impact. The only time you should be balancing on the ball of your base leg foot, is when you are pivoting to get into the proper foot position in order to deliver your kick in the most effective and efficient manner possible.

Note: In the "Return to Fighting Position #1," your kicking foot will travel approximately 85-degrees from the "Follow Through" position (7) back to its original starting position (8). While your base leg (0) continues to remain at the 0-degree position.

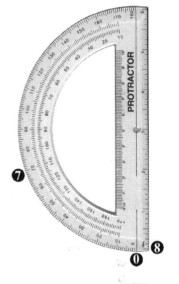

Note: In the "Return to Fighting Position #2," your kicking foot will travel approximately 55-degrees from the "Follow Through" position (7) to another "Fighting Position" (9). However, this time you have stepped forward with your kicking leg rather than returning it to its original starting position as I have illustrated for you above. Your base leg (0) continues to remain at the 0-degree position, although now it will be in the rearward rather than the forward position.

133

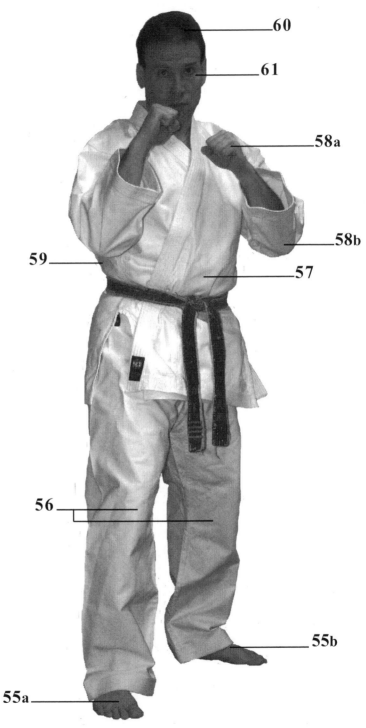

60

61

58a

58b

59

57

56

55b

55a

Return to Fighting Position #2 Front View

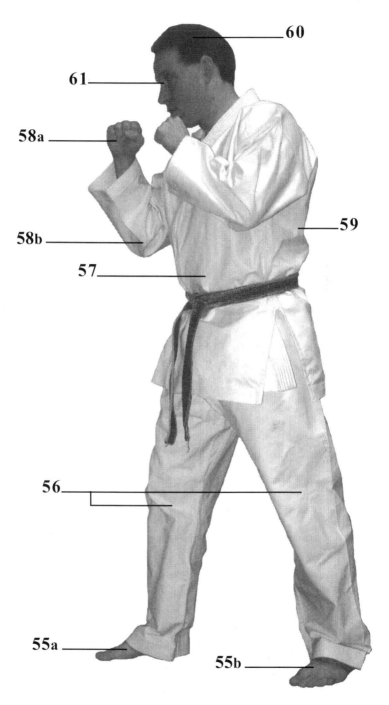

Return to Fighting Position #2 Side View

Pictorial Overview:

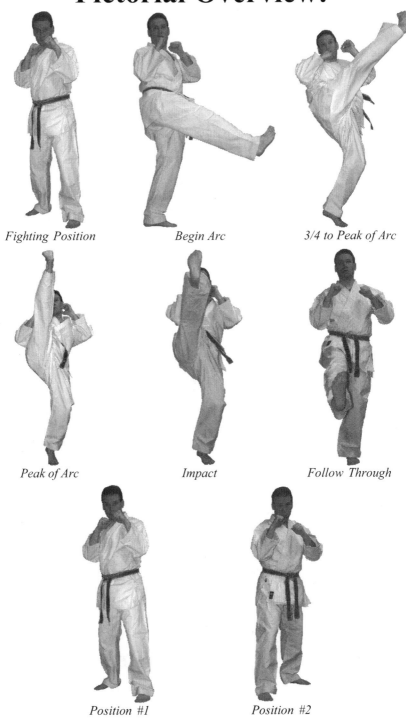

Fighting Position   Begin Arc   3/4 to Peak of Arc

Peak of Arc   Impact   Follow Through

Position #1   Position #2

Note: The illustration below is a visual overview from a "front" perspective of the upward "Path of Trajectory" that your kicking foot will take from the initial "Fighting Position" to the "Peak of Arc" position when executing an In-to-Out Axe Kick with the right leg.

0. The position of your base leg throughout the execution of the entire kick from start to finish is at the 0-degree position.
1. The position of your kicking leg in its initial "Fighting Position" is at the (negative) 15-degree position.
2. The position of your kicking leg as it moves along its upward "Path of Trajectory" approximately 55-degrees to the "Begin Arc" position at the 70-degree position.
3. The position of your kicking leg as it continues along its upward "Path of Trajectory" approximately 70-degrees more to the "3.4 to Peak of Arc" position at the 140-degree position.
4. The position of your kicking leg as it reaches the "Peak of Arc" position which should be at the 180-degree position.

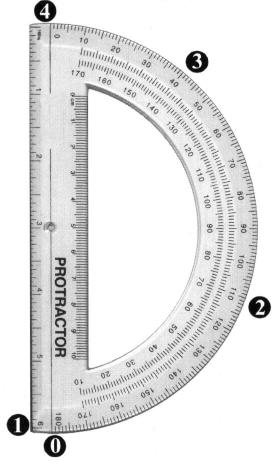

Note: The illustration below is a visual overview from a "side" perspective of the downward "Path of Trajectory" that your kicking foot will take from the "Peak of Arc" position to either one of the two "Return to Fighting Positions" when executing either an Out-to-In Axe Kick or a In-to-Out Axe Kick. This illustration is the same for both the right and left leg.

0. The position of your base leg throughout the execution of the entire kick from start to finish is at the 0-degree position.
5. The position of your kicking leg at the "Peak of Arc" position at the 180-degree position.
6. The position of your kicking leg as it moves along its downward "Path of Trajectory" approximately 40-degrees to the "Impact" position at the 140-degree position.
7. The position of your kicking leg as it continues along its downward "Path of Trajectory" and through its target approximately 70-degrees more to the "Follow Through" position at the 70-degree position.
8. The position of your kicking leg as it returns to its initial "Fighting Position" at the (negative) 15-degree position.
9. The position of your kicking leg if you set it down in front of you instead of behind you in its original starting position.

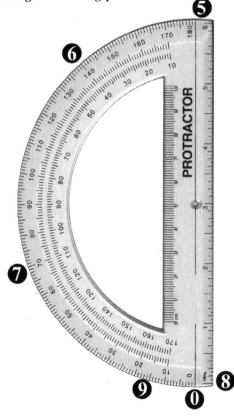

138

Variations of the In-to-Out Axe Kick

This chapter will explain in detail how to properly execute five variations of the In-to-Out Axe Kick. Remember that all of these variations are derived from the co-primary kick In-to-Out Axe Kick. Therefore, it is essential that you learn In-to-Out Axe Kick first before attempting any of these other variations.

To perhaps give you a better understanding of what I mean, let me use the comparison of building a house. Before you start building your house you are first going to need a set of blueprints, this would be the equivalent of the material presented in this book. Next you are going to need the proper materials to begin building with, this would be the equivalent of properly warming-up and stretching before you attempt to practice these kicks.

Next comes the hardest part for students to understand, now in order for your house to be stable, sturdy and secure you must first have a very well built and strong foundation. The foundation of your house is made out of concrete, while the foundation of this particular type of kick is, the In-to-Out Axe Kick. Once you have a strong and proficient In-to-Out Axe Kick, then you can begin to build upon that with the many different variations of that kick. Just like you would build your frame, walls, ceilings, floors and roof of your house.

If you don't take the time to first build a strong and stable foundation, your kicking skills along with your house, will not last and will collapse when the first strong storm or self-defense situation comes along.

As a general rule-of-thumb, every time you practice one of the variations of In-to-Out Axe Kick, you should practice In-to-Out Axe Kick itself at least ten times. I promise you that if you do this, all of your Axe Kicks will steadily improve and become stronger.

Note: Occasionally when executing an Axe Kick, you will find that your kicking foot will not be able to "Follow Through" after impacting with the appropriate vital or vulnerable point on your opponent. Usually, what will end up happening is a "bouncing" effect that will take place immediately after initial impact with your opponent. This takes the form of your leg "bouncing" up after striking your opponent rather than going through your opponent. If and when this happens, do not try and force your kicking foot through the target. Instead, go with the "bounce" and retract your kicking leg immediately by bringing your knee toward your chest while simultaneously bringing your kicking foot back toward your body by bending your kicking leg knee. This happens on both co-primary kicks and their respective variations.

139

Off-Setting In-to-Out Axe Kick

The Off-Setting In-to-Out Axe Kick is identical in execution to the In-to-Out Axe Kick, with one notable exception. A quick double step motion to the side (which puts you at a 45-degree angle from your original starting position), which is performed immediately prior to executing the kick. The starting position is the same as In-to-Out Axe Kick, in that your kicking foot is in the rear position. The actual double-step motion of the feet prior to the execution of the kick is performed by first moving the rearward foot and then the forward foot off at a 45-degree angle to the side of your opponent. When executing the double-step motion, be sure and move your rearward foot first, then your forward foot, without initially moving your hips and upper body in order to avoid telegraphing the move to your opponent. Your hips and upper body will begin to move when you begin to place the forward foot back onto the ground.

Fighting Position:

1. Your fighting position for this kick is exactly the same as it is for Out-to-In Axe Kick, in that your kicking leg will be in the rearward position.
2. This stance is approximately shoulder width apart with the heel of your rear foot directly in line with the heel of your front foot
3. Your front or lead foot should be pointed directly at your opponent.
4. Your rear foot is angled toward the right at approximately a 45-degree angle. Your weight should be distributed evenly over the balls of both feet.
5. Your knees are slightly, but not noticeably bent. They should not be locked straight or rigid.

*Fighting Position
Foot Position*

Fighting Position Front View

Fighting Position Side View

140

6. Your body should be facing at a 45-degree angle toward your opponent. This presents a smaller target area and also facilitates a faster off-set, which in turn allows you the opportunity to initiate a faster kick.

7. Your hands should be held up (like a boxer's), with the elbows tucked in to protect the ribs and your hands up to protect your head. Your hands should remain as close to this position as possible throughout the entire kick.

8. Your head should be facing your opponent with your chin tucked down and protected by your lead shoulder.

9. Your eyes should be centered on your opponent's chest.

Off-Set (part one):

10. Move your rear foot to the right (approximately 2-3 feet), and slightly forward (approximately 8 to 10 inches).

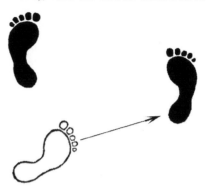

Off-Set Foot Position (part one)

First Step on Off-Set Front View

First Step on Off-Set Side View

Off-Set (part two):

11. Move your front foot to the right approximately 12 to 18 inches. Your body should now be in a Fighting Position at a 45-degree angle from its original starting position.

Off-Set Foot Position (part two)

141

Begin Arc:

12. Using the toes of your kicking foot, while simultaneously pivoting approximately 45-degrees (counterclockwise) on the ball of your base leg foot, push off the floor and bring your kicking leg up and across the front of your body and at approximately a 45-degree angle to the front of your opponent. Your leg should be straight, and your kicking foot should already be in the correct position to strike your opponent.

Begin Arc
Foot Position

Second Step on Off-Set Front View

Second Step on Off-Set Side View

Begin Arc Front View

Begin Arc Side View

142

13. As your bring your kicking leg up, your upper body should now be facing at a slight angle toward your opponent and leaning back slightly. In this position, the kicking leg side of your body will be closer to your opponent than your base leg side. Your back will remain straight but not rigid.

14. Although your hands have switched position, they should still be held up (like a boxer's), with the elbows tucked in to protect the ribs and your hands up to protect your head.

15. Your head is up and facing towards your opponent, while your eyes remain in contact with your opponent throughout the entire kick.

3/4 to Peak of Arc:

16. Your base leg foot should still be in approximately the same position, with your base leg knee being slightly bent. Your kicking leg has now moved up to your opponent's head height, although it is still across the front of your body and at a 45-degree angle to the front of your opponent.

3/4 to Peak of Arc Foot Position

17. Your kicking foot remains in the correct striking position throughout the entire sequence.

18. Your upper body is now facing towards your opponent and leaning back slightly.

19. Although your body is in the above position, your back remains straight but not rigid, and your head should still be facing toward your opponent. Eye contact with your opponent is maintained at all times.

3/4 to Peak of Arc Front View   *3/4 to Peak of Arc Side View*

143

Peak of Arc:

20. Your base leg foot should still be in approximately the same position, with your base leg knee being slightly bent. Your kicking leg has now moved up to the correct height to begin its downward trajectory.
21. The heel of the kicking foot should follow a straight line of trajectory from the "Peak of Arc" through the target (Impact), to the "Follow Through" position.
22. Your upper body should now be facing at a slight angle towards your opponent, while continuing to lean back slightly. In this position, the kicking leg side of your body will be closer to your opponent than your base leg side.
23. Although your body is in the above position, your back remains straight but not rigid, and your head should still be facing towards your opponent. Eye contact with your opponent is maintained at all times.

Peak of Arc
Foot Position

Note: Eventually, after you have become proficient executing the "off-set" movement and the kick independently of one another, you will want to combine the two separate movements together into one continuous movement.

Peak of Arc Front View   *Peak of Arc Side View*

Impact:

24. Your entire base leg foot should now be in contact with the ground and gripping it, while in approximately the same position.

25. Your upper body, with the kicking leg side of your body remaining closer to your opponent than your base leg side, should still be facing at a slight angle towards your opponent, while continuing to lean back slightly. At the moment of impact, your entire body should tighten to add power to the kick, as your foot continues to travel on a downward trajectory through the target.

26. Notice how your kicking foot, kicking leg, hips, back, shoulders and head are all in alignment at the initial moment of "Impact." Also, notice how the toes of the kicking foot are pulled back towards your body and pointed up. This helps insure that contact with the target is made with the back of the heel.

27. Your head should still be facing towards your opponent. Eye contact with your opponent is maintained at all times.

Impact
Foot Position

Note: A sharp exhalation of air or KIAA!, should be executed at the initial moment of impact in order to assist in tightening your body, which in turn will help add power to your kick.

Impact Front View

Impact Side View

145

Follow Through:

28. Your entire base leg foot should remain in contact with the ground and gripping it, while in approximately the same position. The knee on your base leg will remain slightly bent.

29. Your upper body, with the kicking leg side of your body remaining closer to your opponent than your base leg side, should still be facing at a slight angle toward your opponent, while continuing to lean back slightly.

Follow Through Foot Position

30. Your kicking leg foot should continue along exactly the same downward path it followed from the "Peak of Arc" to "Impact." Your foot should now be at approximately knee level.

31. Your head should still be facing towards your opponent. Eye contact with your opponent is maintained at all times.

Note: If you execute an Axe Kick properly, you will exert a minimal amount of muscular effort on the upward "Path of Trajectory" going from the initial "Fighting Position" all the way up to the "Peak of Arc." You will exert the maximum amount of muscular effort on the downward "Path of Trajectory" from the "Peak of Arc" to "Impact" and continuing through to the "Follow Through" position.

Follow Through Front View   *Follow Through Side View*

146

Return to Fighting Position:
There are two ways that you can return to a fighting position from the "Follow Through" position. They are as follows:

32a. After you have reached the "Follow Through" position, simply bring your kicking foot behind you and set it down into a fighting position with your kicking leg behind you, rather than in front of you.

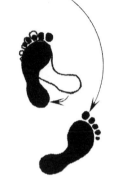

Position #1

32b. After you have reached the "Follow Through" position, simply leave your kicking foot in front of you and set it down into a fighting position with your kicking leg in front of you, rather than behind you.

Position #2

Note: All of these Return to Fighting Position positions, will be at a 45-degree angle to the right of your initial fighting position.

Note: If you want to learn how to improve your strategic thinking, learn not only how to play the game of chess, but also how to study the game of chess.

Note: The available vital and/or vulnerable points that are going to be open to attack on your opponent, is going to be determined by your opponent. However, you can create your own openings on your opponent not only by setting him up with various attack strategies (like a boxer utilizing the jab to set up a right cross or hook), but also by correctly utilizing deception prior to, and during your attack.

147

Pictorial Overview:

Fighting Position   *Off-Set (part one)*   *Off-Set (part two)*

Begin Arc   *3/4 to Peak of Arc*   *Peak of Arc*

Impact   *Follow Through*

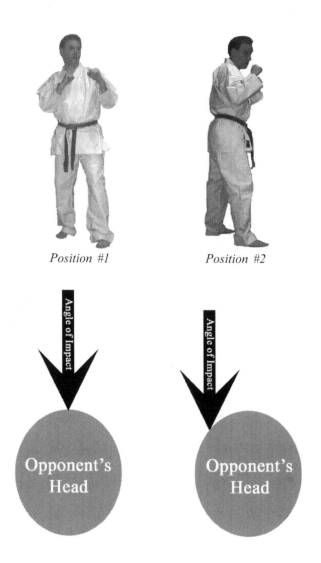

Position #1   *Position #2*

Note: As you can see in the illustrations presented above, if you were to strike your opponent's head with an Axe Kick, the optimum angle for impact in relation to your opponent's head is on the direct center line which would dissect your body into two equal pieces along the vertical plane. Therefore, the further away you are from direct center, the less effective your kick is going to be. For example, as you look at the illustrations above, imagine that you have a front view of your opponent's head. The black arrows are Axe Kicks delivered to the top of your opponent's skull. Which one is going to be more effective, the one on the left? Or the one on the right? The example on the right is incorrect, and more of a "glancing" blow, while the example on the left is correct and a lot more effective.

Cross-Over In-to-Out Axe Kick

The Cross-Over In-to-Out Axe Kick is identical in execution to the In-to-Out Axe Kick, with one notable exception. A cross-over forward motion, which is performed immediately prior to executing the kick. This motion is used to close the distance between your and your opponent, and also to misdirect or deceive your opponent in order to increase your chances of successfully executing the kick. It can also increase the power in this kick due to the added momentum of crossing-over forward. The actual cross-over motion is performed by stepping forward and across your lead foot with your rear foot, while your rear foot remains stationary except for a short counterclockwise pivot on the ball of the foot. The cross-over can be anywhere from a few inches to approximately your shoulder width. Keep your hips and upper body as still as possible throughout the initial cross-over in order to avoid telegraphing the move to your opponent.

Fighting Position:

1. Your fighting position for this kick is exactly the same as it will be for Switch Axe Kick. With your kicking leg in the forward position to begin with rather than in the rearward position.

2. This stance is approximately shoulder width apart with the heel of your rear foot in a direct line with the heel of your front foot.

3. Your front or lead foot should be pointing directly at your opponent.

4. Your rear foot is angled toward the left at approximately a 45-degree angle. Your weight should be distributed evenly

Fighting Position Foot Position

Fighting Position Front View

Cross-Over

Fighting Position Side View

150

over the balls of both feet.

5. Your knees are slightly, but not noticeably bent. They should not be locked straight or rigid.

6. Your body should be facing at a 45-degree angle toward your opponent. This presents a smaller target area and also facilitates a faster cross-over forward, which allows you the opportunity to initiate a faster kick.

7. Your hands should be held up (like a boxers), with the elbows tucked in to protect the ribs and your hands up to protect your head. Your hands should remain as close to this position as possible throughout the entire kick.

8. Your head should be facing your opponent with your chin tucked down and protected by your lead shoulder.

9. Your eyes should be centered on your opponent's chest.

Cross-Over:

10. Keeping your upper body and hips as still as possible, step forward and across the front of your lead leg foot with your rear leg foot. When you place your rear foot back down on the ground, it should be angled toward the left at approximately a 45-degree angle. As soon as the ball of your rear foot touches the ground, begin to execute the kick.

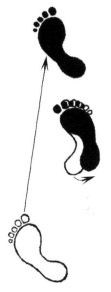

Cross-Over Foot Position

Cross-Over Front View

Cross-Over Side View

151

Begin Arc:

11. Using the toes of your kicking foot, push off the floor and bring your kicking leg up and across the front of your body and at approximately a 45-degree angle to your opponents right. Your leg should be straight, and your kicking foot should already be in the correct position to strike your opponent.

12. As your bring your kicking leg up, your upper body should now be facing at a slight angle toward your opponent and leaning back slightly. In this position, the kicking leg side of your body will be closer to your opponent than your base leg side. Your back will remain straight but not rigid.

13. Although your hands have switched position, they should still be held up (like a boxer's), with the elbows tucked in to protect the ribs and your hands up to protect your head.

14. Your head is up and facing towards your opponent, while your eyes remain in contact with your opponent throughout the entire kick.

Begin Arc Foot Position

Note: One of the practice techniques that I use to develop flexibility and accuracy when executing an Axe Kick, is to perform straight legged Rising Kicks directly to the front while maintaining the same straight vertical line of trajectory on both the upward and downward "Paths of Trajectory."

Begin Arc Front View   *Begin Arc Side View*

152

3/4 to Peak of Arc:

15. Your base leg foot should still be in approximately the same position, with your base leg knee being slightly bent. Your kicking leg has now moved up to your opponent's head height, although it is still across the front of your body and at a 45-degree angle to your opponents right.

16. Your kicking foot remains in the correct striking position throughout the entire sequence.

17. Your upper body is now facing towards your opponent and leaning back slightly.

18. Although your body is in the above position, your back remains straight but not rigid, and your head should still be facing toward your opponent. Your eyes should continue to remain in contact with your opponent throughout the entire kick.

*3/4 to Peak of Arc
Foot Position*

Note: Not only does following the correct upward "Path of Trajectory" by utilizing a big arcing motion create more power, but it also allows you to avoid having your kicking leg grabbed by your opponent and/or your kicking leg blocked by your opponent's legs. Always remember, the shortest distance between point A and point B may not always be the quickest, safest, or most efficient.

3/4 to Peak of Arc Front View   *3/4 to Peak of Arc Side View*

153

Peak of Arc:

19. Your base leg foot should still be in approximately the same position, with your base leg knee being slightly bent. Your kicking leg has now moved up to the correct height to begin its downward trajectory.

20. The heel of the kicking foot should follow a straight line of trajectory from the "Peak of Arc" through the target (Impact), to the "Follow Through" position.

21. Your upper body should now be facing at a slight angle towards your opponent, while continuing to lean back slightly. In this position, the kicking leg side of your body will be closer to your opponent than your base leg side.

22. Although your body is in the above position, your back remains straight but not rigid, and your head should still be facing towards your opponent. Eye contact with your opponent is maintained at all times.

Peak of Arc
Foot Position

Note: **Ideally, while you are momentarily at the "Peak of Arc" position, the entire front of your kicking leg from the junction where the leg fits into the hip all the way up to your kicking heel, should be in a straight vertical line and flush against your upper torso and kicking shoulder.**

Peak of Arc Front View

Peak of Arc Side View

Impact:

23. Your entire base leg foot should now be in contact with the ground and gripping it, while in approximately the same position.

24. Your upper body, with the kicking leg side of your body remaining closer to your opponent than your base leg side, should still be facing at a slight angle towards your opponent, while continuing to lean back slightly. At the moment of impact, your entire body should tighten to add power to the kick, as your foot continues to travel on a downward trajectory through the target.

Impact
Foot Position

25. Notice how your kicking foot, kicking leg, hips, back, shoulders and head are all in alignment at the initial moment of "Impact." Also, notice how the toes of the kicking foot are pulled back towards your body and pointed up. This helps insure that contact with the target is made with the back of the heel.

26. Your head should still be facing towards your opponent. Eye contact with your opponent is maintained at all times.

Note: Because the force generated during the execution of an Axe Kick works against the natural bending motion of the knee. You must pay particular attention to increasing the stretching and strengthening exercises for the muscles and tendons that surround the knee, in order to protect it from incurring any damage during the execution of an Axe Kick.

Impact Front View   *Impact Side View*

Follow Through:

27. Your entire base leg foot should remain in contact with the ground and gripping it, while in approximately the same position. The knee on your base leg will remain slightly bent.

28. Your upper body, with the kicking leg side of your body remaining closer to your opponent than your base leg side, should still be facing at a slight angle toward your opponent, while continuing to lean back slightly.

Follow Through Foot Position

29. Your kicking leg foot should continue along exactly the same downward path it followed from the "Peak of Arc" to "Impact." Your foot should now be at approximately knee level.

30. Your head should still be facing towards your opponent. Eye contact with your opponent is maintained at all times.

Note: Due to its unique nature, and the extremely vulnerable position you are put in during the initial upward "Path of Trajectory," I feel that the Axe Kick is best suited as a finishing technique after your opponent is already "set-up" by another technique, injured, or already on the ground.

Follow Through Front View   *Follow Through Side View*

Return to Fighting Position:
There are two ways that you can return to a fighting position from the "Follow Through" position. They are as follows:

31a. After you have reached the "Follow Through" position, simply leave your kicking foot in front of you and set it down into a fighting position with your kicking leg in front of you, rather than behind you.

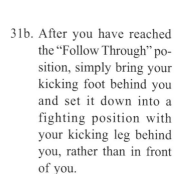

Position #1

31b. After you have reached the "Follow Through" position, simply bring your kicking foot behind you and set it down into a fighting position with your kicking leg behind you, rather than in front of you.

Position #2

Note: The upward "Path of Trajectory" of an Axe Kick, can be likened to the initial upward climb of a roller coaster. While the actual "Peak of Arc" is exactly like that instant of "hang time" that you experience just before the roller coaster begins its downward plummet. Although admittedly, the "hang time" for an Axe Kick at the "Peak of Arc" will be infinitely shorter, while the downward plummet or "Path of Trajectory" from the "Peak of Arc" to the "Follow Through" position, will be infinitely faster than that of the roller coaster.

157

Pictorial Overview:

Fighting Position *Cross-Over* *Begin Arc*

3/4 to Peak of Arc *Peak of Arc* *Impact*

Follow Through *Position #1* *Position #2*

158

Hop/Slide Forward In-to-Out Axe Kick

The Hopping/Sliding Forward In-to-Out Axe Kick is identical in execution to the In-to-Out Axe Kick, with one notable exception. A hopping/sliding forward motion, which is performed immediately prior to executing the kick. This motion is used to close the distance between you and your opponent. It can also increase the power in this kick due to the added momentum of hopping/sliding forward. The actual hop or slide motion is performed by both feet simultaneously moving forward keeping the same distance between them. The hop or slide can be anywhere from a few inches up to 18 inches. Keep your hips and upper body as still as possible throughout the initial hop or slide forward in order to avoid telegraphing the move to your opponent.

Fighting Position:

1. Your fighting position for this kick is exactly the same as it is for In-to-Out Axe Kick. With your kicking leg in the rearward position to begin with rather than in the forward position.

2. This stance is approximately shoulder width apart with the heel of your rear foot in a direct line with the heel of your front foot.

3. Your front or lead foot should be pointing directly at your opponent.

4. Your rear foot is angled toward the right at approximately a 45-degree angle. Your weight should be distributed evenly over the balls of both feet.

5. Your knees are slightly, but not noticeably bent. They should not be locked straight or rigid.

6. Your body should be facing at a 45-degree angle toward your opponent. This presents a smaller target area and

Fighting Position
Foot Position

Fighting Position Front View

Fighting Position Side View

159

also facilitates a faster hop/slide forward, which in turn allows you the opportunity to initiate a faster kick.

7. Your hands should be held up (like a boxers), with the elbows tucked in to protect the ribs and your hands up to protect your head. Your hands should remain as close to this position as possible throughout the entire kick.

8. Your head should be facing your opponent with your chin tucked down and protected by your lead shoulder.

9. Your eyes should be centered on your opponent's chest.

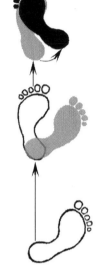

Hop/Slide Forward & Begin Arc:

10. Moving on the balls of your feet, move both feet forward approximately 3 to 18 inches, utilizing a hopping/sliding motion. As you are completing the hop/slide forward, you will begin to execute the kick.

11. Using the toes of your kicking foot, while simultaneously pivoting approximately 45-degrees (counterclockwise) on the ball of your base leg foot, push off the floor and bring your kicking leg up and across the front of your body and at approximately a 45-degree angle to your opponents right. Your leg should be straight, and your kicking foot should already be in the correct position to strike your opponent.

12. As your bring your kicking leg up, your upper body

Hop/Slide Forward &
Begin Arc
Foot Position

Hop/Slide Forward &... Front View   *Hop/Slide Forward &... Side View*

160

should now be facing at a slight angle toward your opponent and leaning back slightly. In this position, the kicking leg side of your body will be closer to your opponent than your base leg side. Your back will remain straight but not rigid.

13. Although your hands have switched position, they should still be held up (like a boxer's), with the elbows tucked in to protect the ribs and your hands up to protect your head.

14. Your head is up and facing towards your opponent, while your eyes remain in contact with your opponent throughout the entire kick.

3/4 to Peak of Arc:

15. Your base leg foot should still be in approximately the same position, with your base leg knee being slightly bent. Your kicking leg has now moved up to your opponent's head height, although it is still across the front of your body and at a 45-degree angle to your opponents right.

16. Your kicking foot remains in the correct striking position throughout the entire sequence.

17. Your upper body is now facing towards your opponent and leaning back slightly.

3/4 to Peak of Arc Foot Position

18. Although your body is in the above position, your back remains straight but not rigid, and your head should still be facing toward your opponent. Your eyes should continue to remain in contact with your opponent throughout the entire kick.

3/4 to Peak of Arc Front View

3/4 to Peak of Arc Side View

161

Peak of Arc:

19. Your base leg foot should still be in approximately the same position, with your base leg knee being slightly bent. Your kicking leg has now moved up to the correct height to begin its downward trajectory.

Peak of Arc Foot Position

20. The heel of the kicking foot should follow a straight line of trajectory from the "Peak of Arc" through the target (Impact), to the "Follow Through" position.

21. Your upper body should now be facing at a slight angle towards your opponent, while continuing to lean back slightly. In this position, the kicking leg side of your body will be closer to your opponent than your base leg side.

22. Although your body is in the above position, your back remains straight but not rigid, and your head should still be facing towards your opponent. Eye contact with your opponent is maintained at all times.

Note: Initially, you will execute the hop or slide forward separately from the Axe Kick. However, after you have become proficient at executing both the hop/slide forward and the In-to-Out Axe Kick separately, you will then combine the two so that as you hop or slide forward, you are already bringing your leg up to the "Peak of Arc" position.

Peak of Arc Front View

Peak of Arc Side View

Impact:

23. Your entire base leg foot should now be in contact with the ground and gripping it, while in approximately the same position.

24. Your upper body, with the kicking leg side of your body remaining closer to your opponent than your base leg side, should still be facing at a slight angle towards your opponent, while continuing to lean back slightly. At the moment of impact, your entire body should tighten to add power to the kick, as your foot continues to travel on a downward trajectory through the target.

*Impact
Foot Position*

25. Notice how your kicking foot, kicking leg, hips, back, shoulders and head are all in alignment at the initial moment of "Impact." Also, notice how the toes of the kicking foot are pulled back towards your body and pointed up. This helps insure that contact with the target is made with the back of the heel.

26. Your head should still be facing towards your opponent. Eye contact with your opponent is maintained at all times.

Note: You must learn to control the bodies innate response to pull back or slow down when it is about to impact with something.

Note: Don't over-extend your technique by "reaching" for your opponent. Create the proper distance using footwork before executing your kick.

Impact Front View

Impact Side View

163

Follow Through:

27. Your entire base leg foot should remain in contact with the ground and gripping it, while in approximately the same position. The knee on your base leg will remain slightly bent.

28. Your upper body, with the kicking leg side of your body remaining closer to your opponent than your base leg side, should still be facing at a slight angle toward your opponent, while continuing to lean back slightly.

Follow Through Foot Position

29. Your kicking leg foot should continue along exactly the same downward path it followed from the "Peak of Arc" to "Impact." Your foot should now be at approximately knee level.

30. Your head should still be facing towards your opponent. Eye contact with your opponent is maintained at all times.

Note: As I mentioned previously on page 79, there is a big difference between kicking in gi pants and barefoot and kicking in everyday clothes and shoes. This is even more apparent when executing an Axe Kick. Try executing and Axe Kick dressed in jeans or dress pants and shoes, or if you are a woman, executing an Axe Kick in a dress and high heels. Notice the difference! There are many variables that need to be factored into a self-defense scenario long before it ever becomes a potential reality. What you are or aren't wearing is just one of them.

Follow Through Front View   *Follow Through Side View*

Return to Fighting Position:
There are two ways that you can return to a fighting position from the "Follow Through" position. They are as follows:

31a. After you have reached the "Follow Through" position, simply bring your kicking foot behind you and set it down into a fighting position with your kicking leg behind you, rather than in front of you.

Position #1

31b. After you have reached the "Follow Through" position, simply leave your kicking foot in front of you and set it down into a fighting position with your kicking leg in front of you, rather than behind you.

Position #2

Note: Unlike the Hop/Slide Forward Axe Kick, the hopping or sliding motion of the Hop/Slide Backward Axe Kick (which begins on page 167), will initially remain separate from the actual kick itself. This is primarily due to the fact that your momentum, which is initially moving backwards, has to stop altogether in order for you to reverse direction in order to execute the kick. However, as you become more proficient at executing both portions of this kick independently from one another, you will eventually combine them into one fluid motion. You will find that as the ball of your back foot touches the ground, you will "push off" with that foot in order to immediately change directions and begin initiating the kick. While at the same time your front foot plants itself firmly in front. This is not easy to do and takes time, patience, and lots of correct practice.

Pictorial Overview:

Fighting Position

Hop/Slide Forward

Begin Arc

3/4 to Peak of Arc

Peak of Arc

Impact

Follow Through

Position #1

Position #2

166

Hop/Slide Backward In-to-Out Axe Kick

The Hopping/Sliding Backward In-to-Out Axe Kick is identical in execution to the In-to-Out Axe Kick, with one notable exception. A hopping/sliding backward motion, which is performed immediately prior to executing the kick. This hopping/sliding backward motion is used to draw your opponent into you, or to avoid an attack. It can also increase the power in this kick due to the added momentum of hopping/sliding backward. The actual hop or slide motion is performed by both feet simultaneously moving backward keeping the same distance between them. The hop or slide can be anywhere from a few inches up to 18 inches. Keep your hips and upper body as still as possible throughout the initial hop or slide backward in order to avoid telegraphing the move to your opponent.

Fighting Position:

1. Your fighting position for this kick is exactly the same as it is for In-to-Out Axe Kick. With your kicking leg in the rearward position to begin with rather than in the forward position.
2. This stance is approximately shoulder width apart with the heel of your rear foot in a direct line with the heel of your front foot.
3. Your front or lead foot should be pointing directly at your opponent.
4. Your rear foot is angled toward the right at approximately a 45-degree angle. Your weight should be distributed evenly over the balls of both feet.
5. Your knees are slightly, but not noticeably bent. They should not be locked straight or rigid.

Fighting Position Foot Position

Fighting Position Front View

Fighting Position Side View

167

6. Your body should be facing at a 45-degree angle toward your opponent. This presents a smaller target area and also facilitates a faster hop/slide backward, which in turn allows you the opportunity to initiate a faster kick.

7. Your hands should be held up (like a boxers), with the elbows tucked in to protect the ribs and your hands up to protect your head. Your hands should remain as close to this position as possible throughout the entire kick.

8. Your head should be facing your opponent with your chin tucked down and protected by your lead shoulder.

9. Your eyes should be centered on your opponent's chest.

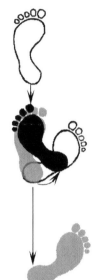

Hop/Slide Backward & Begin Arc:

10. Moving on the balls of your feet, move both feet forward approximately 3 to 18 inches, utilizing a hopping/sliding motion. As you are completing the hop/slide forward, you will begin to execute the kick.

11. Using the toes of your kicking foot, while simultaneously pivoting approximately 45-degrees (counterclockwise) on the ball of your base leg foot, push off the floor and bring your kicking leg up and across the front of your body and at approximately a 45-degree angle to your opponents right. Your leg should be straight, and your kicking foot should already be in the correct position to strike your opponent.

Hop/Slide Backward & Begin Arc Foot Position

Slide/Hop Back & Begin Arc Front View   *Slide/Hop Back & Begin Arc Side View*

12. As your bring your kicking leg up, your upper body should now be facing at a slight angle toward your opponent and leaning back slightly. In this position, the kicking leg side of your body will be closer to your opponent than your base leg side. Your back will remain straight but not rigid.

13. Although your hands have switched position, they should still be held up (like a boxer's), with the elbows tucked in to protect the ribs and your hands up to protect your head.

14. Your head is up and facing towards your opponent, while your eyes remain in contact with your opponent throughout the entire kick.

3/4 to Peak of Arc:

15. Your base leg foot should still be in approximately the same position, with your base leg knee being slightly bent. Your kicking leg has now moved up to your opponent's head height, although it is still across the front of your body and at a 45-degree angle to your opponents right.

16. Your kicking foot remains in the correct striking position throughout the entire sequence.

17. Your upper body is now facing towards your opponent and leaning back slightly.

3/4 to Peak of Arc Foot Position

18. Although your body is in the above position, your back remains straight but not rigid, and your head should still be facing toward your opponent. Your eyes should continue to remain in contact with your opponent throughout the entire kick.

3/4 to Peak of Arc Front View   *3/4 to Peak of Arc Side View*

Peak of Arc:

19. Your base leg foot should still be in approximately the same position, with your base leg knee being slightly bent. Your kicking leg has now moved up to the correct height to begin its downward trajectory.

20. The heel of the kicking foot should follow a straight line of trajectory from the "Peak of Arc" through the target (Impact), to the "Follow Through" position.

Peak of Arc Foot Position

21. Your upper body should now be facing at a slight angle towards your opponent, while continuing to lean back slightly. In this position, the kicking leg side of your body will be closer to your opponent than your base leg side.

22. Although your body is in the above position, your back remains straight but not rigid, and your head should still be facing towards your opponent. Eye contact with your opponent is maintained at all times.

Note: Looking at the illustrations on the left and on the following three pages, imagine that the block of wood represents your opponent, while the head of the axe represents your kicking foot, and the length of the axe handle representing your kicking leg. As you look...

Peak of Arc Front View   *Peak of Arc Side View*

170

Impact:

23. Your entire base leg foot should now be in contact with the ground and gripping it, while in approximately the same position.

24. Your upper body, with the kicking leg side of your body remaining closer to your opponent than your base leg side, should still be facing at a slight angle towards your opponent, while continuing to lean back slightly. At the moment of impact, your entire body should tighten to add power to the kick, as your foot continues to travel on a downward trajectory through the target.

25. Notice how your kicking foot, kicking leg, hips, back, shoulders and head are all in alignment at the initial moment of "Impact." Also, notice how the toes of the kicking foot are pulled back towards your body and pointed up. This helps insure that contact with the target is made with the back of the heel.

26. Your head should still be facing towards your opponent. Eye contact with your opponent is maintained at all times.

*Impact
Foot Position*

Note: ...at these illustrations, ask yourself the following questions. 1. Can I effectively chop a block of wood using the end of the handle (your butt and hip) rather than the head of the axe (as illustrated on the previous page)? 2. Could I chop through the block of wood...

Impact Front View

Impact Side View

171

Follow Through:

27. Your entire base leg foot should remain in contact with the ground and gripping it, while in approximately the same position. The knee on your base leg will remain slightly bent.

28. Your upper body, with the kicking leg side of your body remaining closer to your opponent than your base leg side, should still be facing at a slight angle toward your opponent, while continuing to lean back slightly.

Follow Through Foot Position

29. Your kicking leg foot should continue along exactly the same downward path it followed from the "Peak of Arc" to "Impact." Your foot should now be at approximately knee level.

30. Your head should still be facing towards your opponent. Eye contact with your opponent is maintained at all times.

Note: ...using the top of the axe (the entire bottom of your foot)? 3. What if I used the handle just below the head of the axe (your achille's tendon and calf), could I chop through the block of wood then?

Follow Through Front View

Follow Through Side View

Return to Fighting Position:
There are two ways that you can return to a fighting position from the "Follow Through" position. They are as follows:

31a. After you have reached the "Follow Through" position, simply bring your kicking foot behind you and set it down into a fighting position with your kicking leg behind you, rather than in front of you.

Position #1

31b. After you have reached the "Follow Through" position, simply leave your kicking foot in front of you and set it down into a fighting position with your kicking leg in front of you, rather than behind you.

Position #2

Note: Utilizing a combination of the correct striking implement (the back of the heel) on the head of the axe, along with the correct technique, striking the precise spot (vital or vulnerable point) on the block of wood, will make chopping through it more efficient and effective.

173

Pictorial Overview:

Fighting Position   *Hop/Slide Backward*   *Begin Arc*

3/4 to Peak of Arc   *Peak of Arc*   *Impact*

Follow Through   *Position #1*   *Position #2*

Switch In-to-Out Axe Kick

The Switch In-to-Out Axe Kick is identical in execution to the In-to-Out Axe Kick, with one notable exception. A switching motion of the feet, which is performed immediately prior to the execution of the kick. The switch is used to confuse the opponent and can also increase the power in this kick due to the added momentum of switching your feet. The starting position is the same as it is for Cross-Over In-to-Out Axe Kick, with your kicking leg in the forward position rather than in the rearward position. The actual switching of the feet prior to execution of the kick is performed by simultaneously switching the position of both feet utilizing a straight line or scissors type motion. With the end result being a fighting position with the kicking leg now in the rearward position. When executing the switch, be sure and move your feet first without initially moving your hips and upper body in order to avoid telegraphing the switch to your opponent. Your hips and upper body will begin to move immediately after your feet, but not before.

Fighting Position:

1. Your fighting position for this kick is exactly the same as it was for Cross-Over In-to-Out Axe Kick. With your kicking leg in the forward position to begin with rather than in the rearward position.

2. This stance is approximately shoulder width apart with the heel of your rear foot in a direct line with the heel of your front foot.

3. Your front or lead foot should be pointing directly at your opponent.

*Fighting Position
Foot Position*

Fighting Position Front View

Fighting Position Side View

175

4. Your rear foot is angled towards the left at approximately a 45-degree angle. Your weight should be distributed evenly over the balls of both feet.
5. Your knees are slightly, but not noticeably bent. They should not be locked or rigid.
6. Your body should be facing at a 45-degree angle toward your opponent. This presents a smaller target area and also facilitates a faster switch, which in turn allows you the opportunity to initiate a faster kick.
7. Your hands should be held up (like a boxer's), with the elbows tucked in to protect the ribs and your hands up to protect your head. Your hands should remain as close to this position as possible throughout the entire kick.
8. Your head should be facing your opponent with your chin tucked down and protected by your lead shoulder.
9. Your eyes should be centered on your opponents chest.

Switch Feet & Begin Arc:

10. Utilizing a scissors type motion of your legs and feet, simultaneously switch your front foot with your rear foot and vice versa. As soon as the ball of your front foot touches the ground in the rearward position, begin to execute the kick.
11. Using the toes of your kicking foot, while simultaneously pivoting approximately 45-degrees (counterclockwise) on the ball of your base leg foot, push off the floor and bring your kicking leg up at approximately a 45-degree angle to your opponents right. Your leg should be straight and your

Switch Feet & Begin Arc Foot Position

Switch Feet & Begin Arc Front View   *Switch Feet & Begin Arc Side View*

kicking foot should already be in the correct position to strike your opponent.

12. As your bring your kicking leg up, your upper body should start turning as it begins to face towards your opponent. Your back will remain straight but not rigid.

13. Although your hands have switched position, they should still be held up (like a boxer's), with the elbows tucked in to protect the ribs and your hands up to protect your head.

14. Your head is up and facing towards your opponent, while your eyes remain in contact with your opponent throughout the entire kick.

3/4 to Peak of Arc:

15. Your base leg foot should still be in approximately the same position, with your base leg knee being slightly bent. Your kicking leg has now moved up to your opponent's head height, although it is still across the front of your body and at a 45-degree angle to your opponents right.

16. Your kicking foot remains in the correct striking position throughout the entire sequence.

17. Your upper body is now facing towards your opponent and leaning back slightly.

18. Although your body is in the above position, your back remains straight but not rigid, and your head should still be facing toward your opponent. Your eyes should continue to remain in contact with your opponent throughout the entire kick.

3/4 to Peak of Arc Foot Position

3/4 to Peak of Arc Front View   *3/4 to Peak of Arc Side View*

177

Peak of Arc:

19. Your base leg foot should still be in approximately the same position, with your base leg knee being slightly bent. Your kicking leg has now moved up to the correct height to begin its downward trajectory.

20. The heel of the kicking foot should follow a straight line of trajectory from the "Peak of Arc" through the target (Impact), to the "Follow Through" position.

Peak of Arc Foot Position

21. Your upper body should now be facing at a slight angle towards your opponent, while continuing to lean back slightly. In this position, the kicking leg side of your body will be closer to your opponent than your base leg side.

22. Although your body is in the above position, your back remains straight but not rigid, and your head should still be facing towards your opponent. Eye contact with your opponent is maintained at all times.

Note: When executing a "Switch" kick of any kind, compare it to the shooting action of a rifle. For example; the switching motion is the trigger on the rifle, while the ground is the firing pin, the ball of your kicking foot is the primer in the bullet casing, the combination of muscular speed, strength and proper technique is the gunpowder, and finally, the heel of your kicking foot is the bullet. As you squeeze the trigger (switch your feet), it releases the firing pin striking the primer in the casing...

Peak of Arc Front View   *Peak of Arc Side View*

Impact:

23. Your entire base leg foot should now be in contact with the ground and gripping it, while in approximately the same position.

24. Your upper body, with the kicking leg side of your body remaining closer to your opponent than your base leg side, should still be facing at a slight angle towards your opponent, while continuing to lean back slightly. At the moment of impact, your entire body should tighten to add power to the kick, as your foot continues to travel on a downward trajectory through the target.

25. Notice how your kicking foot, kicking leg, hips, back, shoulders and head are all in alignment at the initial moment of "Impact." Also, notice how the toes of the kicking foot are pulled back towards your body and pointed up. This helps insure that contact with the target is made with the back of the heel.

26. Your head should still be facing towards your opponent. Eye contact with your opponent is maintained at all times.

*Impact
Foot Position*

Note: ...(the ball of your kicking foot touching the ground), and ignites the gunpowder, which fires the bullet (execute your kick) along its path of trajectory, where it <u>STRIKES THROUGH</u> its target.

Impact Front View

Impact Side View

Follow Through:

27. Your entire base leg foot should remain in contact with the ground and gripping it, while in approximately the same position. The knee on your base leg will remain slightly bent.

Follow Through Foot Position

28. Your upper body, with the kicking leg side of your body remaining closer to your opponent than your base leg side, should still be facing at a slight angle toward your opponent, while continuing to lean back slightly.

29. Your kicking leg foot should continue along exactly the same downward path it followed from the "Peak of Arc" to "Impact." Your foot should now be at approximately knee level.

30. Your head should still be facing towards your opponent. Eye contact with your opponent is maintained at all times.

Note: When delivering an Axe Kick along its downward "Path of Trajectory" from the "Peak of Arc" position through "Impact" and continuing to the "Follow Through" position, you should straighten your slightly bent base leg in order to add more power to your kick. However, do not lock your base leg straight. There should always be a slight bend in the knee.

Follow Through Front View

Follow Through Side View

Return to Fighting Position:
There are two ways that you can return to a fighting position from the "Follow Through" position. They are as follows:

31a. After you have reached the "Follow Through" position, simply bring your kicking foot behind you and set it down into a fighting position with your kicking leg behind you, rather than in front of you.

Position #1

31b. After you have reached the "Follow Through" position, simply leave your kicking foot in front of you and set it down into a fighting position with your kicking leg in front of you, rather than behind you.

Position #2

Note: Eventually, after you have correctly executed thousands of Switch In-to-Out Axe Kicks, there should be little to no change at all in the position of your upper body before, during, or even after you "switch" your feet prior to kicking. As a matter of fact, your upper body should more closely resemble a Cross-Over In-to-Out Axe Kick. Only instead of "crossing-over" your feet, you are "switching" your feet.

Pictorial Overview:

Fighting Position

Switch Feet

Begin Arc

3/4 to Peak of Arc

Peak of Arc

Impact

Follow Through

Position #1

Position #2

182

Switch In-to-Out Axe Kick
(With the left leg)

Here is an example on how to change the instructions presented in this book in order to execute the exact same kicks with the left leg. First of all you're going to be kicking with the left leg rather than the right, so your rear foot and body position will be exactly opposite of those that you would use if you were kicking with the right leg. To put it simply, kicking with the left leg should mirror exactly those kicks performed with the right leg and vice versa.

Fighting Position:

1. Your fighting position for this kick is the exact same as for In-to-Out Axe Kick. However, since you are going to be kicking with the left leg, it will be in the forward position to begin with rather than in the rearward position.
2. This stance is approximately shoulder width apart with the heel of your rear foot in a direct line with the heel of your front foot.
3. Your front or lead foot should be pointing directly at your opponent.
4. Your rear foot is angled towards the right at approximately a 45-degree angle. Your weight should be distributed evenly over the balls of both feet.
5. Your knees are slightly, but not noticeably bent. They should not be locked straight or rigid.
6. Your body should be facing at a 45-degree angle toward

Fighting Position
Foot Position

Fighting Position Front View

Fighting Position Side View

your opponent. This presents a smaller target area and also facilitates a faster switch, which in turn allows you the opportunity to initiate a faster kick.

7. Your hands should be held up (like a boxer's), with the elbows tucked in to protect the ribs and your hands up to protect your head. Your hands should remain as close to this position as possible throughout the entire kick.

8. Your head should be facing your opponent with your chin tucked down and protected by your lead shoulder.

9. Your eyes should be centered on your opponent's chest.

Switch Feet & Begin Arc:

10. Utilizing a scissors type motion of your legs and feet, simultaneously switch your front foot with your rear foot and vice versa. As soon as the ball of your front foot touches the ground in the rearward position, begin to execute the kick.

11. Using the toes of your kicking foot, while simultaneously pivoting approximately 45-degrees (clockwise) on the ball of your base leg foot, push off the floor and bring your kicking leg up at approximately a 45-degree angle to your opponents left. Your leg should be straight, and your kicking foot should already be in the correct position to strike your opponent.

Switch Feet & Begin Arc Foot Position

12. As your bring your kicking leg up, your upper body should start turning as it begins to face towards your opponent. Your back will remain straight but not rigid.

Switch Feet & Begin Arc Front View　　　*Switch Feet & Begin Arc Side View*

184

13. Although your hands have switched position, they should still be held up (like a boxer's), with the elbows tucked in to protect the ribs and your hands up to protect your head.
14. Your head is up and facing towards your opponent, while your eyes remain in contact with your opponent throughout the entire kick.

3/4 to Peak of Arc:

15. Your base leg foot should still be in approximately the same position, with your base leg knee being slightly bent. Your kicking leg has now moved up to your opponent's head height, although it is still across the front of your body and at a 45-degree angle to your opponents left.
16. Your kicking foot remains in the correct striking position throughout the entire sequence.
17. Your upper body is now facing towards your opponent and leaning back slightly.

3/4 to Peak of Arc Foot Position

18. Although your body is in the above position, your back remains straight but not rigid, and your head should still be facing toward your opponent. Your eyes should continue to remain in contact with your opponent throughout the entire kick.

Note: As your are bringing your kicking foot up to the "Peak of Arc" position, do not get into the bad habit of leaning forward. Always keep your back straight during the upward "Path of Trajectory."

3/4 to Peak of Arc Front View   *3/4 to Peak of Arc Side View*

Peak of Arc:

19. Your base leg foot should still be in approximately the same position, with your base leg knee being slightly bent. Your kicking leg has now moved up to the correct height to begin its downward trajectory.

20. The heel of the kicking foot should follow a straight line of trajectory from the "Peak of Arc" through the target (Impact), to the "Follow Through" position.

21. Your upper body should now be facing at a slight angle towards your opponent, while continuing to lean back slightly. In this position, the kicking leg side of your body will be closer to your opponent than your base leg side.

22. Although your body is in the above position, your back remains straight but not rigid, and your head should still be facing towards your opponent. Eye contact with your opponent is maintained at all times.

*Peak of Arc
Foot Position*

Note: When delivering an Axe Kick along its downward "Path of Trajectory" from the "Peak of Arc" position through "Impact" and continuing to the "Follow Through" position, you should lean slightly, but not too far, back in order to add more power to your kick.

Peak of Arc Front View   *Peak of Arc Side View*

Impact:

23. Your entire base leg foot should now be in contact with the ground and gripping it, while in approximately the same position.

24. Your upper body, with the kicking leg side of your body remaining closer to your opponent than your base leg side, should still be facing at a slight angle towards your opponent, while continuing to lean back slightly. At the moment of impact, your entire body should tighten to add power to the kick, as your foot continues to travel on a downward trajectory through the target.

25. Notice how your kicking foot, kicking leg, hips, back, shoulders and head are all in alignment at the initial moment of "Impact." Also, notice how the toes of the kicking foot are pulled back towards your body and pointed up. This helps insure that contact with the target is made with the back of the heel.

26. Your head should still be facing towards your opponent. Eye contact with your opponent is maintained at all times.

Impact
Foot Position

Note: **The head, which can easily be compared to the ever popular "bobblehead" dolls, makes for a difficult target with a kick due to the ease in which the head can "bob and weave" like a boxer in order to avoid being hit.**

Impact Front View   *Impact Side View*

187

Follow Through:

27. Your entire base leg foot should remain in contact with the ground and gripping it, while in approximately the same position. The knee on your base leg will remain slightly bent.

28. Your upper body, with the kicking leg side of your body remaining closer to your opponent than your base leg side, should still be facing at a slight angle toward your opponent, while continuing to lean back slightly.

*Follow Through
Foot Position*

29. Your kicking leg foot should continue along exactly the same downward path it followed from the "Peak of Arc" to "Impact." Your foot should now be at approximately knee level.

30. Your head should still be facing towards your opponent. Eye contact with your opponent is maintained at all times.

Note: Although I have broken down all of the kicks in this book into various steps, you must remember that eventually you will be executing these kicks without thought in one fluid motion while adhering to every principle and technique described in this book in order to maximize the effectiveness of your kick.

Follow Through Front View   *Follow Through Side View*

Return to Fighting Position:
There are two ways that you can return to a fighting position from the "Follow Through" position. They are as follows:

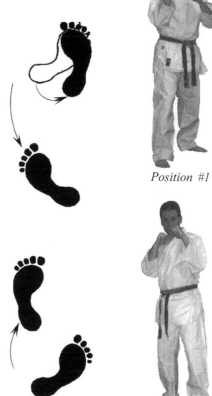

31a. After you have reached the "Follow Through" position, simply bring your kicking foot behind you and set it down into a fighting position with your kicking leg behind you, rather than in front of you.

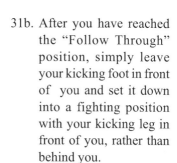

Position #1

31b. After you have reached the "Follow Through" position, simply leave your kicking foot in front of you and set it down into a fighting position with your kicking leg in front of you, rather than behind you.

Position #2

Note: One of the many exercises that I do in order to improve my kicking ability, is to try and execute as many kicks as I can correctly before setting my kicking foot back down on the ground. This exercise not only improves your kicking ability, but it is also a great way to improve your balance and your foot/eye coordination.

Pictorial Overview:

Fighting Position   *Switch Feet*   *Begin Arc*

3/4 to Peak of Arc   *Peak of Arc*   *Impact*

Follow Through   *Position #1*   *Position #2*

190

Training and Practice Methods

The following practice methods in this section, when performed correctly and consistently, are designed to improve your skill, speed, and power when executing an Axe Kick. However, whether or not you improve is dependent solely upon you and your commitment to your training. When performing the exercises and drills that follow, concentrate on form and technique rather than speed or power.

Skill

The precise movement and skill you wish to obtain in the ring and on the street should be practiced correctly and consistently during training.

In other words, how you practice and train in the dojo is how you will react in the ring or on the street.

Kicking skills must be practiced correctly and consistently or speed and technique will begin to deteriorate.

Your kicking skills can be likened to an automobile. With proper maintenance and care, your automobile will last a lifetime. However, if you neglect it, your automobile will break down on you when you need it most. Since you never can tell when you will suddenly need those skills, you should strive to not only maintain them, but also to constantly improve them. Now let's take a look at some of my favorite training exercise that I use in order to improve my Axe Kick.

Mirror & Tape:

The mirror is without a doubt my favorite training aid. It enables me to see myself clearly and analyze my technique in minute detail. I can then correct any flaws as they become evident.

Take two pieces of colored tape (for obvious reasons), and put them on the mirror vertically (the entire length of the mirror) and parallel to each other about 8 to 10 inches apart. Roughly the width of your own head. Now you can practice your Axe Kicks by bringing them up to the "Peak of Arc" position, and then bringing them down in a straight line between the two pieces of tape without telegraphing the kick. This is a fantastic way to improve your Axe Kicks and one that I strongly recommend you perform at the beginning of every workout.

Training Partner:

Training with a partner is an invaluable way to practice as a partner can tell you if you are making a mistake when executing your kick. Partners can also hold bags and pads for kicking, as well as, making the entire work out more enjoyable. A word of caution though, if your training partner spends a good deal of time talking and less time working out, then perhaps it is time to search for a new partner. Idle chatter should have no place in your training regimen. A focused workout session on your own is infinitely preferable to one spent with a poor partner.

Wall Practice:

This exercise to improve my Axe Kick was first demonstrated to me over twenty years ago. It is still valid today and should be an important part of your training program. This exercise is very simple to perform and focuses primarily on building strength and power during the impact, strike through, and follow through, phases of the Axe Kick. Start by placing your back squarely against a wall. Keeping your hands up in a fighting position, have your training partner grab your kicking foot by the heel as you bring your kicking leg up to approximately waist level. Once your training partner has your foot firmly in their grasp, have them slowly raise your leg up to approximately their head level. Once you have reached this point, slowly push down with your kicking leg against your training partners hands as he provides resistance against your downward force. Your partner should not be a immovable force during this exercise, but rather provide a variable form of resistance depending upon your own personal level of strength and flexibility. **Remember**, keep both legs straight throughout this exercise.

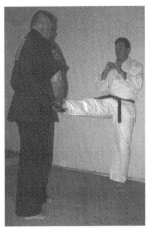  

Starting Position   *Impact*   *Strike Through*

Follow Through   *Finishing Position*

Another variation of this exercise, is to use it as a form of partner stretching. To do this, start by placing your back squarely against a wall. Keeping your hands up in a fighting position, have your training partner grab your kicking foot by the heel as you bring your kicking leg up to approximately waist level. Once your training partner has your foot firmly in their grasp, have them slowly raise your leg up until you can no longer go any higher. Hold it for 5 to 10 seconds, then have your partner slowly lower your leg down to the ground. Repeat this stretch with the other leg. **Remember**, do not resist on this exercise, relax and stretch.

Starting Position

Slowly raise your...

...partners kicking leg...

...as high as it can safely go before ...

...returning it to the Starting Position

193

Strength

Nearly every movement in the martial arts is carried out in opposition to a resistance. Therefore, an increase in strength means an improvement in performance.

"Stronger muscles give the athlete greater movement potential. If everything is equal, the stronger athlete will be bigger, faster, more flexible, more enduring, and less prone to injury." —Dr. Ellington Darden

"One of the benefits of strength is that it acts as a shock absorber for a muscle. Most injuries, such as tennis elbow, are caused by a force or succession of forces that cause the muscle to exceed its tensile strength. When that happens, the muscle tears. The stronger you are, the less likely that is to happen." —Michael Quinn

In order to increase muscular strength and endurance, the muscles must be worked harder than normal.

Your legs carry you everywhere you go, and are approximately 10 times stronger than your arms. Therefore the stronger your legs are, the stronger you are.

Although I have included only a few specific leg exercises in this volume, I consider the following exercises to be some of the best available for adding strength to not only your Axe Kicks, but all of your other kicks as well. In subsequent volumes in the Achieving Kicking Excellence series, I will include several additional leg exercises which, depending on how you perform them, can develop either strength or endurance depending on the amount of weight used and repetitions performed. As with all exercises, train hard, but train smart.

Squats-with weights:

Squats are perhaps the single best overall strength building exercise there is for the entire body, and most assuredly the best exercise there is for the lower body. The muscles emphasized during the squat are the quadriceps, gluteus maximus, lower back and the hamstrings. Ideally you should use a squat rack and training partner every time you perform this exercise. However, not all of us have access to a health club or weight training facility. Therefore the utmost in caution must be exercised when lifting weights by yourself. You should never lift heavy weights without someone present to spot for you. Always wear shoes, weight lifting gloves and a weight lifting belt for support when you are weight lifting.

Before you begin, make sure that the weighted plates are securely fastened to the end of the bar. It is also a good idea to have a padded wrap around the center portion of the bar, where it rests across the back of your shoulders during the execution of this exercise. Bending your knees and keeping your back straight, squat down and grasp the bar with a comfortable grip. Your legs should be approximately shoulder width apart with your toes pointed slightly outward. Straighten your legs to a standing position while lifting the bar up to your chest. Press the bar over your head and then carefully lower it behind your neck until it is resting on the back of your shoulders as seen in the starting position.

From this position, slowly bend your legs, allowing your knees to move outward in the same direction as your toes. At the same time contract your back muscles in order keep your body rigid as your perform this exercise. Slowly squat down until

194

you are in a full squat position with your thighs parallel to the ground. Once you have reached the full squat position, slowly stand up to the starting position. Repeat this movement as often and as safely as you can.

Remember:

1. Keep your back straight throughout the entire movement.
2. Focus your eyes on a spot at head level in order to help keep your head up.
3. Do not bounce at the bottom of the squat.
4. Do not squat lower than your thighs parallel to the floor.
5. Do not use heavy weights without a squat rack and spotters present.

Training Routine:

1. For strength use a heavier weight and perform three sets of 8 to 12 repetitions.
2. For endurance use a lighter weight and perform three to five sets of 15 to 20 repetitions per set.
3. Perform this exercise no more than 3 times per week.

Starting & Finishing Position *Squat Position*

195

Hack Squat Machine:

Squats are perhaps the single best overall strength building exercise there is for the entire body, and most assuredly the best exercise there is for the lower body. The muscles emphasized during the squat are the quadriceps, gluteus maximus, lower back and the hamstrings. The Hack Squat is a variation of the basic squat, and is an excellent means of isolating the leg muscles. This exercise is used by many weightlifters when they have no spotter available, or when they can no longer safely perform free weight squats because their back or legs are too tired or sore. Remember, you should always wear shoes, weight lifting gloves and a weight lifting belt for support when you are weight lifting.

Before you begin, make sure that the weighted plates are securely fastened to the machine. Step into the machine and place your back against the padded surface, while wedging your shoulders beneath the padded yokes attached to the front of the machine. Your legs should be straight and your feet should be approximately 6 to 10 inches apart and parallel with each other. Firmly grasp the handles located on the sides of the machine. Keeping your back straight, reach down and release the safety bar.

From this position, slowly bend your legs, allowing your knees to move outward in the same direction as your toes. At the same time contract your back muscles in order keep your body rigid as your perform this exercise. Slowly squat down until you are in a full squat position with your thighs parallel to the ground. Once you have reached the full squat position, slowly stand up to the starting position. Repeat this movement as often and as safely as you can. This exercise primarily emphasizes the quadriceps. However, if you place your feet closer together, you will place more emphasis on the gluteal muscles. If you spread your feet further apart, you will place more emphasis on the adductors.

Remember:

1. Keep your back straight throughout the entire movement.
2. Focus your eyes on a spot at head level in order to help keep your head up.
3. Do not bounce at the bottom of the squat.
4. Do not squat lower than your thighs parallel to the foot, or base plate.
5. Inhale as you are performing the squat, and exhale as you are straightening your legs.

Training Routine:

1. For strength use a heavier weight and perform three sets of 8 to 12 repetitions.
2. For endurance use a lighter weight and perform three to five sets of 15 to 20 repetitions per set.
3. Perform this exercise no more than 3 times per week.

196

Starting & Finishing Position

Squat Position

197

Inclined Leg Press:

The Inclined Leg Press is another variation of the standard squat, which places little to no pressure on the back. Therefore, if you have back problems which preclude you from executing a standard squat, you can use this exercise as a substitute. The muscles emphasized during the leg press are the same as they are for the squat, they are the quadriceps, gluteus maximus, and the hamstrings. This exercise is used by many weightlifters when they have no spotter available, or when they can no longer safely perform free weight squats because their back or legs are too tired or sore. Remember, you should always wear shoes, weight lifting gloves and a weight lifting belt for support when you are weight lifting.

Before you begin, make sure that the weighted plates are securely fastened to the machine. Step into the machine and sit down placing your back against the padded surface, while placing your butt on the padded seat. Your legs should be straight and your feet should be approximately shoulder width apart and parallel with each other. Firmly grasp the handles located on the sides of the machine. Keeping your legs straight, reach down and release the safety bar.

From this position, slowly bend your legs, allowing your knees to move slowly towards your chest. As your knees move toward your chest, make sure that they move to the outside of your chest and not directly at the chest itself. Once your knees have reached the appropriate distance from your chest, press your legs upward and return to the starting position. Repeat this movement as often and as safely as you can. Placing your feet low on the plate or closer together, primarily emphasizes the quadriceps. However, if you place your feet farther apart, you will place more emphasis on the adductors. If you place your feet high on the plate, you will place more emphasis on the gluteals and hamstrings.

Remember:

1. **Using too heavy of a weight can cause damage to the hip and pelvic area.**
2. As with all exercises, exhale during the execution of the movement, and inhale as you return to your original starting position.
3. Do not raise your butt up, always keep your butt on the padded seat!
4. Do not lower the weight too close to your chest before pressing upward.
5. Do not bounce at the top or bottom of the movement.

Training Routine:

1. For strength use a heavier weight and perform three sets of 8 to 12 repetitions.
2. For endurance use a lighter weight and perform three to five sets of 15 to 20 repetitions per set.
3. Perform this exercise no more than 3 times per week.

Starting Position

Leg Press Position

199

Cable Machine Axe Kicks:

This exercise places primary emphasis on the gluteus maximus and, to a lesser extent, the hamstrings. This exercise can be performed on any dual-cable weight machine with an overhead lat attachment. Select the desired weight you can comfortably work with, yet is still challenging. Before you begin, make sure that the ankle strap is securely attached to your ankle. It is also a good idea to have a thick sock on so that the ankle strap doesn't rub against your leg during the execution of this exercise. Start the exercise by first standing facing the cable machine with your back straight. Grasp the handle on the metal bar located above and between the dual-machines for balance. Keep your back straight and your weight centered over your base leg, raise your opposite leg straight up and in front of you and attach the cable to the ankle strap (you may require assistance with this). This will be the starting and finishing position for this exercise. Keeping your leg straight, lower your leg back down to the ground. Once your foot touches the ground, slowly and carefully raise your leg back to the starting position. Repeat this movement as often and as safely as you can.

Remember:
1. Perform this exercise slowly in order to obtain the maximum benefit.
2. Do not do partial movements. Utilize the entire range of motion on this exercise.

Training Routine:
1. Use light weights to start with and perform three to five sets of 25 to 30 repetitions per set.
2. Perform this exercise no more than 3 times per week.

Starting & Finishing Position   *Axe Kick Position*

Lunges with weights:

This exercise places primary emphasis on the gluteus maximus and, to a lesser degree, the quadriceps and hamstrings. Begin by standing with your feet approximately shoulder width apart and your toes pointed forward. Keeping your back straight, squat down and lift the barbell up and place it behind your head and across your shoulders. Your hands should maintain a wide grip on the bar for better balance. Keep your back straight and your head up throughout the entire exercise. From this position, slowly step forward approximately two and a half to three shoulder widths. Once you have reached the forward lunge position, your forward leg thigh should be parallel with the floor, while your rear leg is straight. The entire bottom surface of both feet should be flat on the ground. Slowly return to the starting position, and repeat this movement on the opposite side. Repeat this movement as often and as safely as you can. **DO NOT** use heavy weights on this exercise!

Remember:

1. Keep your back straight and your head up throughout the entire movement.
2. As you lunge forward, put all of your body weight on your forward leg

Training Routine:

1. This is primarily an endurance building exercise and should be performed with a high number of repetitions (30 to 100) for several sets (3 to 10).
2. Perform this exercise no more than 3 times per week.

Starting & Finishing Position

Lunge Forward w/One Leg

Return to Starting Position

Lunge Forward w/Other Leg

201

Lunges without weights:

This exercise, along with the variation using weights described on page 201, is perhaps one of the best overall leg exercises that you can do in order to improve both strength and flexibility in your legs for kicking, especially when executing an Axe Kick. Begin by standing with your feet approximately shoulder width apart and your toes pointed forward. Your hands can be either behind your head, or resting on your hips. Keep your back straight and your head up throughout the entire exercise. From this position, slowly step forward approximately two and a half to three shoulder widths. Once you have reached the forward lunge position, your forward leg thigh should be parallel with the floor, while your rear leg is straight. The entire bottom surface of both feet should be flat on the ground. Hold this position for a moment, then slowly return to the starting position. Once you return to the starting position, repeat this movement on the opposite side. Repeat this movement as often and as safely as you can.

Remember:

1. Keep your back straight throughout the entire movement.
2. Focus your eyes on a spot at head level in order to help keep your head up.
3. Do not bounce at the bottom of the forward lunge.
4. Do not squat lower than your front thigh parallel with the floor.

Training Routine:

1. This is primarily an endurance building exercise and should be performed with a high number of repetitions (30 to 100) for several sets (3 to 10).
2. Perform this exercise no more than 3 times per week.

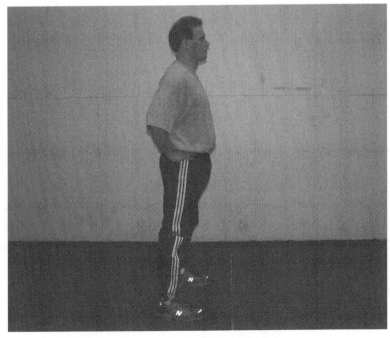

Starting & Finishing Position

Lunge Position with the Left Leg Forward

Lunge Position with the Right Leg Forward

203

Duck Walking:

Begin by standing with your feet approximately shoulders width apart and your toes pointing forward. Keeping your back straight and your head up, bring your arms up into a fighting position with your hands at shoulder level. From this position, slowly squat down until your thighs are parallel with the ground. Once you have reached the squat position, duck walk (step) forward with one leg. After you have placed your foot down in front of you, step forward with the other leg. Just like your were walking normally, only in this case you are walking forward while in the squat position. Repeat this movement as often and as safely as you can.

Remember:

1. Keep your back straight and rigid throughout the entire movement.
2. Focus your eyes on a spot at head level in order to help keep your head up.
3. Always keep your thighs parallel with the floor.
4. **This exercise places a lot of stress on the knee, therefore use extreme caution while performing this exercise.**

Training Routine:

1. This is primarily an endurance building exercise and should be performed with a high number of repetitions per leg (30 to 100), for several sets (3 to 10).
2. Perform this exercise no more than 3 times per week.

Starting & Finishing Position

Squat Down

Step Forward w/One Leg

Step Forward w/Other Leg

204

Plyometric High Knee Raises:

Plyometric high knee raises are without a doubt one of the best exercises to perform in order to add explosive power to your kicks. This exercise emphasizes all of the muscles of the leg to a certain degree, from the muscles of the foot all the way up to the gluteus maximus and lower back. When performing this or any other plyometric type exercise, you should exercise extreme caution due to the amount of stress that is placed on your body from these exercises. I would advise you to perform these exercises no more than two times per week, and to give yourself at least two days rest in between each plyometric training routine. Before you begin, make sure that the area around you is clear of any obstacles.

This exercise can be performed with or without shoes. Make sure that you are wearing gi bottoms or other loose fitting pants. Begin by standing with your feet approximately shoulders width apart and your toes pointing forward. Keeping your back straight and your head up, bring your arms up into a fighting position with your hands at shoulder level. From this position, explosively bring one of your knees up as high as you can to your upper chest. As soon as your knee reaches your chest, explosively force your leg back down to the ground, but don't slam your foot into the ground. Set it down gently, but quickly. As soon as your foot touches the ground, immediately and explosively repeat the same movement with your opposite leg. Repeat this movement as often and as safely as you can alternating your legs each time.

Remember:

1. Make sure that the area around you is free of any obstacles.
2. Focus your eyes on a spot at head level in order to help keep your head up.
3. Do not slam your foot into the ground. Set it down quickly, but gently.
4. Your back should be kept as straight as possible at all times.
5. Do not perform plyometric type exercises more than twice per week.

Training Routine:

1. Perform one set of 10 to 20 repetitions per leg, no more than 2 times per week.
2. Work up to two sets of 20 to 50 repetitions per leg, no more than 2 times per week.

Starting Position

High Knee Position

Return to Starting Position

High Knee Position

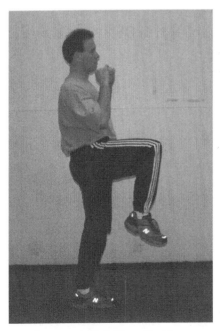

Incorrect High Knee Position

206

Speed

The speed of your kicks during training should be at the same speed you plan to use during self-defense or during competition.

As I stated earlier in this section, how you practice and train in the dojo is how you will react in the ring or on the street.

The primary component of speed under pressure is not physical, but mental. Therefore, you must stay focused and concentrate.

Your mind controls your body; you must therefore keep control of your mind in order to perform at your optimum level.

If you think that you're slow, you will be slow. If however you believe that you can be faster, you will be faster.

Now let's take a look at some of my favorite speed training exercises that I use to increase the speed in my Axe Kicks.

Ankle Weights:

This is my favorite piece of exercise equipment that I use in order to improve the speed of not only my Axe Kicks, but all other kicks as well. Properly used ankle weights can improve your speed and hitting power in your legs as well as increasing muscular stamina. Improperly used however, they can cause a variety of injuries to the joints and connective tissues. This is not only detrimental to your body, but it also causes you to lose valuable training time. When practicing your kicks with ankle weights, you should make sure that they are securely fastened around your ankles and not loose. Start with 2 lbs. on each ankle and gradually build up the weight over time. Don't rush it. Perform your kicks no faster than 3/4 speed. Concentrate on technique and form. Remember that your legs will weaken faster utilizing the ankle weights. Therefore caution must be exercised so that you do not injure your knees or hips. Any kicking drill or exercise can be utilized with the ankle weights, with the notable exceptions of plyometric exercises and reactionary drills. I do not recommend using any kind of weight when performing plyometric exercises. These exercises are of such high intensity that no additional weight is needed. Reactionary drills require you to kick as fast as you can in response to an outside stimulus. Therefore ankle weights would be a hindrance rather than a benefit.

Quick Draw:

This is an excellent reactionary drill and requires the use of a training partner. I got the idea of this training method from watching western movies when I was a kid. Picture the following scene from any western movie.

The sheriff looks out the window of the saloon onto the dust-covered Main Street of town where the outlaw who killed his father stands waiting. A tied down six-gun slung low on his right thigh. The sheriff steps through the saloon doors and out onto the porch, his eyes never leaving the outlaw. He walks off the porch and out onto the street where he turns toward the outlaw. They stand facing each other from no more than 50 feet. Neither one moves. Suddenly the outlaw makes a move for his gun. BANG! The outlaw falls backward, dead, a .45 caliber bullet lodged in his brain. The sheriff holsters his Colt Peacemaker and walks back into the saloon.

Now you may be asking yourself how is this going to help your kicking skills. The answer is really quite simple. I have modified the classic western shoot out, or quick draw, by utilizing a training partner and your kicks instead of a Colt Peacemaker. Begin by having your training partner stand in front of you out of kicking range. You will be facing him in a fighting position. At your partner's discretion, he will make a prearranged movement, which will be the indicator for you to execute a kick as quickly as you can toward your partner. That indicator can be anything from a snapping of the fingers to the blinking of an eye. Use your imagination. Kicks can be performed one at a time, two or three at a time, using the same leg or alternating legs. Be creative and design your own unique routine. This exercise can also be utilized with a force bag or kicking paddle. However, extreme care must be utilized so that you do not accidentally miss your target and end up hitting your training partner. That doesn't seem to go over to well with training partners.

Water Training:

This particular training method requires a rather large piece of training equipment, a full-sized swimming pool. The deep end of the pool needs to be at least 6 feet deep in order for you to practice your kicks in mid-chest to shoulder deep water. This method of practicing your kicking technique is identical to performing the two co-primary kicks and all of their variations in the air. However, always keep in mind that when you are practicing in water, you will always be kicking against a constant state of resistance.

Start off by practicing your kicking technique at 1/4 speed until your kicking skills become easier and more natural. As you become progressively more efficient in your kicking skills, you will gradually increase your speed until you are performing your kicks at full speed. Remember, as you approach the "3/4 to Peak of Arc" position, your kicking foot will exit the water and will not reenter the water until shortly after the "Impact" phase of the kick. Use this to your advantage by focusing on both the exiting of your kicking foot from the water and its subsequent reentry. Make both the exit and reentry as fast and as explosive as possible. Even though you are practicing in the water, never sacrifice proper technique for speed or power.

It is imperative that you take all necessary precautions when practicing this technique. If at all possible, utilize this training method only with a training partner in case of any unforeseen accidents.

Jump Rope:

Jumping rope is not only a time-honored method for building endurance in the sport of boxing, but it is also an excellent method of building rhythmic foot movement and speed for all sports that require foot and hand coordination.

Proper Repetitive Practice:

Regardless of the activity, the more you practice the faster you will become, provided proper technique is maintained throughout the exercise. Notice the difference in the speed of your kick from the very first time you practice it, to the 1,000th time, the 5,000th time, the 10,000th time, etc. Which one was faster?

Power

Force = Mass x Acceleration

In other words, the faster you are, multiplied by the greatest amount of muscular mass that you can generate behind your kick, equals striking power. Now let's take a look at my two favorite pieces of training equipment that I utilize in order to improve my kicking power when executing an Axe Kick. They are the force bag (hand held kicking shield) and the kicking paddle.

Force Bag:

The force bag or kicking shield is a hand held pad or bag, that is usually made out of vinyl or leather with a foam filled core. There are usually two sets of handles located on the bag, two on the back portion of the bag, and one on each side of the bag. If utilized correctly, these bags are invaluable as training aids in order to increase the speed and power in your Axe Kicks.

Begin by having your bag holder grasp the handles located on the sides of the bag. He should hold the bag straight out in front of him (with arms above his head), and parallel with the ground, with the top of the force bag at your head height. He should position himself in a parallel stance with his legs about one and a half to two shoulder widths apart. As the kicker, you want to aim your kicks about 4 inches in from the closest edge of the bag, and at the center of the bag (which represents the top center of your opponents head), where the vital/vulnerable points you are striking at are located. At all times you must be extremely careful when kicking so that you do not accidentally kick your training partner. They tend to get a little grouchy when kicked.

As the bag holder, you do not want to get in the habit of being just a bag holder. Utilize this time to improve your defensive skills by relaxing your body the entire time until just before the moment of impact. Make sure that the bottom edge of the bag is parallel to the ground and facing directly at the kicker at his head height. It should not be at an angle. You can utilize any kicking routine you can think of with the force bag. You can practice single kicks, multiple kicks (one leg at a time or alternating legs), the Quick Draw method, etc. You are only limited by your own imagination.

Kicking Paddle:

The kicking paddle is a very versatile piece of training equipment that, when utilized correctly, can help improve not only the power in your Axe Kick, but also your accuracy, speed, timing, and footwork. Another benefit of training with the kicking paddle is to help you to improve your ability to obtain and maintain the correct kicking distance between you and your opponent. Because it offers so much versatility in your training routine, the kicking paddle can also be used to simulate the offensive and defensive movements of an actual opponent.

You can utilize full force Axe Kicks on the kicking paddles without worrying about damaging them. However, when using the kicking paddle or any other piece of training equipment, you must exercise caution so that you don't inadvertently hurt yourself by hyper-extending your knee, twisting an ankle, etc., or hurting your training partner by inadvertently hitting him or her. This is why the kicking paddle consists of the handle and the separate target area. Strike the target area when kicking, not the hands of your training partner. There are numerous routines, which you can utilize when working with the kicking paddle. Some of the routines I utilize in order to improve my Axe Kicks are exactly the same as those utilized when kicking the force bag. While other routines are designed to simulate actual sparring conditions.

Running:

Running is a must for anyone who is serious about self-defense or competition. I will not go into any details about running itself other than to say that it should be an essential part of any martial artists training program. There are several good books on running available, and any one of them would be an invaluable addition to your library.

Running Stairs:

In addition to regular running, running stairs is an excellent method of building the muscles in the legs while at the same time building up your aerobic capacity and endurance. However, extreme caution must be exercised at all times to avoid injuring yourself while performing this or any exercise described in this book.

Relaxation and Tension:

Muscle contractions used during training should duplicate those used in self-defense or competition.

If you do not utilize the proper tension and relaxation principles in the dojo when kicking, you will not use them correctly on the street or in the ring. This principle is very simple yet seems to be very difficult for individuals to follow. Physiologically speaking a relaxed muscle is able to react faster than a tense muscle. Therefore, you want to remain as relaxed as possible from the time you initiate your kick until just before the moment of impact. At this point your entire body should tighten up to add power to your kick. Immediately after the moment of impact, your muscles should once again relax in order to facilitate a faster "Follow Through" after impact with your target. I have found that the best method for practicing this technique is to perform the Water Training method, which I described earlier in this section. Perform this technique slowly and concentrate on proper technique while remaining totally relaxed throughout the kicking process until just before the moment of impact. At this point tighten all of the muscles in your body and hold them that way for just an instant. **Remember,** once impact has been made, relax immediately and complete your kick.

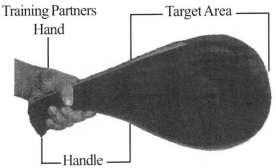

Training Partners Hand ⎯ Target Area ⎯

⎯ Handle ⎯

Kicking Paddle

Trouble Shooting Guide

In this chapter, I will present some of the most common questions concerning mistakes that I have encountered from students when attempting to perform the Out-to-In/In-to-Out Axe Kick or any one of their many variations. I will then attempt to provide a generalized answer to each of those questions. Although one must keep in mind that there is no way to provide the appropriate answer to each person without actually seeing him or her perform the kick in person. When you have a problem, always refer back to the instruction section that covers that particular movement in which you are having a problem. One of my instructors once imparted upon me a small piece of wisdom that I would now like to share with you concerning mistakes. "If you suddenly find yourself making mistakes, go back to the beginning." In other words, you can never practice or study the basic techniques enough, for they are the foundation in which all other techniques are based.

Why do I always seem to be hitting with the wrong part of my foot?
This is usually caused by one of three things. (1) You are not bringing your toes back and towards your shin exposing the back of your heel as the striking implement. This happens quite often when one tries "reaching" for the target, rather than having already created the proper striking distance. (2) Or, as I briefly mentioned in number one, you may even be too far away from your opponent and trying to "reach" for the target by extending your kicking foot towards your opponent, which would result in a strike with the toes or ball of your foot instead of the back of the heel. (3) You are too close to your opponent prior to executing the Axe Kick and you end up striking your opponent with the back of your calf or Achille's heel, rather than the back of the heel. Remember to always create the proper striking distance before you execute your kick, not during the execution of the kick.

Why does it seem that I can never get my leg up high enough to deliver an effective Axe Kick?
This particular problem is almost exclusively caused by one thing, lack of flexibility. You may need to focus a lot more time on stretching not only your legs, but also your hips and lower back. Unfortunately, you may be one of those people that no matter what you do, you just won't ever be able to obtain the high degree of flexibility needed to execute an Axe Kick on a standing 6'5" inch person. That's okay because you don't need to. Simply utilize another technique to make your opponent bend over and/or hit the ground. Now's the time to drop an Axe Kick on him!

Every time I try and use an Axe Kick with a training partner, they always seem to see it coming and move out of the way!
This particular problem can be related not only to improper technique, but also to inappropriate use of the Axe Kick. Let's look at technique first. (1) You may not be "coiling" fast enough prior to execution of the technique, or you may be making some unconscious body movement prior to executing the kick, and therefore are

telegraphing your intentions to you opponent. (2) Another possible problem is that you may not yet have the entire sequence of movements flowing together to where they are all one continuous motion. You may be pausing during the execution of the kick and not be aware of it. The best way to correct both of these problems is to practice in front of a mirror. (3) The other possibility is that your technique is fine, but your application of the kick is incorrect. Are you attempting to use the Axe Kick as your initial technique? Or as a finishing technique? Remember that for the most part, the Axe Kick is a finishing technique rather than an initial technique, although it can effectively be used in both instances. Try limiting your use of the kick when sparring and always try and set up the Axe Kick by utilizing another technique before executing it. Whether it is another kick, punch or even simply footwork.

My Axe Kick always seems to glance off the target, or get caught by my opponent, whether it's in a tournament or in the dojo!

This is a very easy problem to correct, remember that an Axe Kick, for the most part, is very easy to see coming and if your kick is slow, it will be easy to grab or avoid. Two other points to remember, (1) you must strike the correct vulnerable/vital point at the correct angle with the correct striking implement. (2) You are "telegraphing" your Axe Kick prior to executing it. Therefore, you need to "set-up" the Axe Kick with another technique first before attempting to use it.

Why do my Axe Kicks miss the target more times that they hit it?

The most common solution to this problem is that you have to make sure that you are creating the correct distance between you and your opponent prior to executing the kick. Another possibility may be that you need to practice the downward "Path of Trajectory" portion of the kick more often and slower until your accuracy improves.

It seems like every time I hit my opponent, that my kick "bounces" off him with little to no apparent effect!

This can most often be attributed to a person hitting with a "surface strike" on his opponent, rather than "striking through" his opponent. In order to correct this you need to work on three primary areas. (1) A faster "Follow Through" with the kicking leg faster after impact. (2) Practicing the tension and relaxation movements before, during and after impact. (3) Striking the correct vulnerable/vital point on your opponent with the correct striking implement.

I can do an In-to-Out Axe Kick and Out-to-In Axe Kick fairly well, but when it comes to some of the other Axe Kicks, I always seem to have problems!

The important thing to remember here is that all of the Axe Kick variations are based on either of the two co-primary kicks (Out-to-In Axe Kick and In-to-Out Axe Kick). If you are executing the two co-primary kicks correctly, then you need to focus more of your attention on not only the additional moves associated with each

212

particular variation, but also in the ability to flow in a continuous motion from the additional portion of each particular Axe Kick variation, to either the Out-to-In Axe Kick or the In-to-Out Axe Kick.

Why do I lose my balance every time I kick?
There are several possible reasons for this. (1) You may not be keeping your head up and looking at your opponent while executing the kick. (2) You may be attempting to imitate a bird by waving your arms all over the place instead of having them in control and next to your body. (3) Your center of gravity may not be over your base leg. (4) Over-extending the kicking leg. (5) Leaning to far backward with your upper body during the execution of the kick. (6) Balancing on the ball of your foot rather than the entire base foot when kicking.

How come I just can't seem to get any power into my Axe Kick?
Power in an Axe Kick is generated by the correct execution of all phases of the kick and by gravity. The most important being proper technique. For arguments sake, let us assume (and you know what happens when you make an assumption) that you are performing all of the "movement" phases of the kick correctly. I would then have to say that you are probably not performing the tension and relaxation portion of the kick correctly, as this is the most difficult aspect of the kick to perform correctly. Remember that the entire body should be in a relaxed state throughout the entire execution of the kick, except immediately before impact. When the entire body should turn into a solid, rigid mass to support and add power to the kick, and then immediately relax again to add speed to the recovery or "Follow Through." Another possible reason is that you need to get your kicking leg up higher at the "Peak of Arc" position.

Why is my Axe Kick so slow?
Anything is slow the first few hundred or even a thousand times you do them. Speed is not important to learning, be patient and practice until the kick becomes instinctive in nature. After you become comfortable with the execution of the kick, then you can gradually add more speed when executing it. If you are still experiencing a slow kick, you may be too tense when executing the kick and this will greatly decrease your speed. Another potential problem could be that you "see" yourself as being slow. If you want to be fast, think fast!

Why do I always seem to land off-balance?
There are several possible reasons for this, and it may be a combination of these instead of just one. (1) You are over-extending "reaching" with your kicking leg. (2) Your center of gravity is not over your base leg. (3) You are trying to execute the kick while balancing on the ball of your base foot rather than the entire foot itself.
Remember that often times we are unable to see clearly are own mistakes. That is why a qualified and competent instructor, and a good training partner is so vitally important to your martial arts training.

213

Axe Kick Applications

In this chapter, I will discuss some of the basic applications for the Out-to-In and In-to-Out Axe Kicks and the ten variations discussed in this book. Please keep in mind that the numerous applications of each kick could fill an entire book. Therefore, I will limit this section to one application per kick. A second series of books detailing the combat and tournament applications of each kick is in the works and will be published following the release of this ten volume series. Keep in mind that the photographs in this section are staged in order to give you the best possible view of each technique in order to help you learn from them. The actual execution of any of these kicks should be instantaneously (without thought), and in one continuous motion. My assistant and I have intentionally made some errors that can be seen in some of these photographs in order to help you correct some common mistakes. See if you can spot them before I tell you them at the end of each kicking application.

For reference purposes, Ron Dunlap will be the attacker while I will be the defender in this series of photographs. Ron is wearing a black uniform, while I am wearing a white uniform.

Out-to-In Axe Kick:

1. You and your opponent are facing each other in what is commonly referred to as a Closed Position, meaning that each of you has the same leg forward and the front of your bodies facing in different directions. In this photograph, both Ron and I have our left legs forward, while the front of Ron's body is basically facing toward the camera, and the front of my body is facing away from the camera.

2. By reading your opponents body language, you discern that he is going to initiate an attack by attempting to grab your leg(s) and wrestle you down to the ground. Immediately, upon sensing this, you begin to initiate your kick.

3. Always make sure to follow the correct upward "Path of Trajectory" arcing motion up to the "Peak of Arc," which should be as high above your opponent's head as possible, before beginning the downward "Path of Trajectory." Remember to protect yourself at all times and not to telegraph your intentions to your attacker.

4. Execute the kick. Ideally you want to strike your opponent when he is midway through his committed technique. By the time your opponents eyes have registered the fact that you have moved your leg, his brain should be registering the pain as your kick connects to the vital or vulnerable point you have just initially struck. Don't forget to "follow through" with your kicking leg after impact.

Did you notice anything wrong or improper in this series of photographs? Take another look. See them now?

First look closely at photograph number two; when you look at Ron's face, you can see that he is looking down at my legs with his eyes rather than having them focused on my chest like a flashlight. This is a very bad habit to get into and one that needs to be broken immediately. Not only does this telegraph your intentions to your opponent, but it may also lead to a punch in the nose while you are looking at your opponent's feet. I, however, as the defender in this situation, have just been presented with a great opportunity for now I know where my opponent plans on attacking.

Now look closely at photograph number three; even though my kicking leg is up fairly high during the "Peak of Arc" position, in this case it isn't up high enough. My kicking leg should be flush against my upper chest and abdomen making a straight vertical line from the heel of my kicking foot to the heel of my base leg foot. The higher you can bring your kicking leg up as you reach the "Peak of Arc" position (while maintaining proper technique), the more potential power that can be generated into the delivery of an Axe Kick.

In-to-Out Axe Kick:

1. Once again, you and your opponent are facing each other in what is commonly referred to as a Closed Position.

2. As soon as you sense a "stutter" in your opponents actions, you immediately begin to execute the kick.

A "stutter" is an indecisive moment when your opponent is unsure of what to do next. This is a momentary hesitation that can be capitalized on by you if you know what to look for and act instantaneously and decisively when it occurs.

3. Correctly execute the upward "Path of Trajectory" to the "Peak of Arc" position. Remember to protect yourself at all times and not to telegraph your intentions to your attacker. As you can see in this photograph, you are in a very dangerous and unstable position. You should strive to have your kick so fast, that you will have completed your kick before you even realize that your foot has left the ground.

4. Execute the kick.

Did you notice anything wrong or improper in this series of photographs? Take another look. See them now?

If you look closely at photograph number four; you will see that I have struck Ron not with the back of my heel, but with the back off my Achille's Tendon and calf muscle. Not exactly the preferred striking implement with any kick, let alone the Axe Kick. **Always** strike the correct vital or vulnerable point on your opponent with the correct striking implement. This not only maximizes the effectiveness of your kick, but it also minimizes the possibility of injury to you.

Switch Out-to-In Axe Kick:

1. You and your attacker are facing each other in what is commonly referred to as an Open Position, meaning that one of you, in this case Ron, has his left leg forward while I have my right leg forward. This will result in both of our bodies facing in the same direction. In this case, the front of both Ron and I are basically facing toward the camera, while our backs are facing away from the camera.

2. Sensing my opponents impending attack, and wishing to confuse him while repositioning my body, I switch the position of my feet utilizing a scissors type motion. This results in my opponent and I now being in a Closed Position.

3. Begin to execute the kick. Remember to maintain eye contact with your attacker.

217

4. One of the many reasons why you want to make a correct "arcing" motion with your leg during the upward "Path of Trajectory," is to avoid the possibility of your opponent grabbing your kicking leg.

5. Execute the kick. Remember, that your kicking leg should never "hang" in the air. Immediately after making impact with your opponent, you should immediately "Follow Through" or retract your kicking leg and get it back down on the ground.

Did you notice anything wrong or improper in this series of photographs? Take another look. See them now?

If you look closely at photograph number five, you can clearly see that although I have struck Ron with an Axe Kick, I did not strike him correctly with the back of my heel, instead I struck Ron with my Achille's tendon and calf muscle. This is not only incorrect, but it also greatly lessens the impact potential of your kick. Along with using the incorrect striking implement, I failed to strike the correct vital or vulnerable point on Ron's head. Instead, I struck the top center of Ron's head, rather than the bregma. Combined with using the incorrect striking implement, not striking the correct vital or vulnerable point even further lessens the impact potential of your kick.

To give you an example; like I have stated throughout this book, "Correctly executing all aspects of an Axe Kick is like explosively splitting a block of wood with an axe." However, not doing so can be likened to trying to chop through a block of wood with a plastic whiffle ball bat. You figure out which one you want to use on an opponent, the axe or the plastic whiffle ball bat.

Off-Setting Out-to-In Axe Kick:

1. You and your opponent are facing each other in an Open Position. Your opponent starts to turn or twist his body in a counterclockwise motion, indicating that he is going to attempt a spinning or turning technique.

2. Seeing that your opponent has committed to his counterclockwise turn or spin, you begin to "off-set" in the same counterclockwise direction. This enables you to move with your opponent and into his blind side where he will not be able to see you.

3. Before your opponent has completed his counterclockwise turn or spin, you should have already completed your "off-setting" motion and...

4. ...begun to execute your kick.

5. While maintaining correct form and technique, raise your kicking leg up as high as possible to the "Peak of Arc" position.

6. Execute the kick. Ideally you want to strike your attacker just before he completes his turn or spin and before his foot is placed firmly back on the ground. This will make your kick even more effective than if you wait to strike your opponent after he has returned to a strong and stable position.

Did you notice anything wrong or improper in this series of photographs? Take another look. See them now?

If you look closely at photograph number two, you can see that I started my off-setting move a little too soon. I should have waited just an instant longer until Ron had firmly committed to his turn and therefore, would have had a more difficult time seeing me. Timing is a very important part of not only self-defense, but also every facet of your daily life. If you have great timing, you will have a lot easier time with almost every activity in your life.

Now look closely at photograph number six, you can clearly see that I have struck Ron on the top of his shoulder. This is correct! Remember, that the main targets that can be effectively struck with an Axe Kick are; the head, neck, spine and shoulders.

Off-Setting In-to-Out Axe Kick:

1. You and your opponent are facing each other in a Closed Position. However, in this case, the front of Ron's body is basically in a squared off position and facing toward me, while the front of my body is facing toward the camera.

2. Your opponent attempts to lunge for your legs in a classic wrestling take down. As soon as you sense your opponent's impending attack, you begin to offset his attack by moving your right foot to the right and at a 45-degree angle to your opponent. Which you immediately follow with...

3. ...moving your left leg to the right to complete the "off-setting" movement. This will effectively move your body out of the line of attack, and puts you in a very advantageous position to initiate a counterattack against your attacker. Remember to keep your hands up and protect yourself at all times.

4. As your left foot completes the "off-setting" movement, you should already begin to execute your kick. Since you are kicking in the direction of your opponents outstretched hands, you must make sure that you are executing your upward "Path of Trajectory" correctly, or you will hit your opponent's arms.

5. Execute the kick. Ideally, you will want to strike your attacker while he is off balance and in a vulnerable position. As seen in this picture. Not only is Ron in a bent over position which leaves the back of his neck and spine in a very vulnerable position, but his center of gravity and balance is now in front of his feet rather than over them. Bad for Ron, but great for me!

Did you notice anything wrong or improper in this series of photographs? Take another look. See them now?

If you look closely at photograph number three, you can see that by making the choice to execute an In-to-Out Axe Kick, I am bringing my kick up in front of my opponent not only where he can clearly see it, but also where he already has his arms outstretched in an attempt to grab my legs. In this particular instance, a better choice would have been to execute an Out-to-In Axe Kick where my kicking leg would have traveled behind Ron where it would have not only been harder for him to see (if at all), but it would also be farther away from his outstretched arms. Which could have potentially grabbed my kicking leg as it traveled along its upward path of trajectory.

This is one of the reasons why it is so important to learn not only **"How"** to kick correctly, but also the **"Who, What, Where, When, and Why"** of kicking. These principles, although discussed briefly in Chapter Three, will be discussed in great detail in an upcoming ten volume series which will focus on the combat and tournament applications of each of the ten primary kicks and their respective variations.

As you look at photograph number five, you can clearly see that I have left my kicking leg "hanging" in the air after striking Ron. Even though your opponent may be in this or any vulnerable position, remember to retract your kicking leg immediately after making contact with your target. Leaving it hang out there reduces the power in your kick and your recovery time. It also presents a very tempting target to your opponent. No matter how fast your kick strikes the target, it should be even faster coming back.

Step-Back Out-to-In Axe Kick:

1. You and your opponent are facing each other in an Open Position. Your opponent attempts to punch you with his right hand. As you can see in this photograph, any attempt to execute an Axe Kick from this position would be to slow and would leave me even more vulnerable to Ron's punch.

2. Therefore, in order to avoid your opponent's punch and put you in a more effective kicking position, you will first step back with your lead leg. This will increase the distance between you and your opponent, which will allow you the opportunity to execute a kick. As soon as your lead leg steps back...

3. ...begin to execute the kick. Remember that you never want to sacrifice technique for speed.

4. Execute the kick.

Did you notice anything wrong or improper in this series of photographs? Take another look. See them now?

If you look closely at photographs number two, three, and four, you can clearly see that Ron has left his arm hanging out in the air after trying to punch me rather than retracting it to the correct on-guard or boxing position. This is bad for Ron, but a great opportunity for me. See how the entire right hand side of Ron's body is open from just below his shoulder all the way down to his ankle. Know what a mistake is, and when your opponent makes one, take advantage of it.

Spin Back Out-to-In Axe Kick:

1. You and your opponent are facing each other in an Open Position. While currently at an effective punching range, you are too close to effectively utilize your kicks.

2. Therefore, in order to create a more effective kicking range and in an attempt to deceive your opponent, you begin to execute a "spin back" motion. Even though you are in effect stepping away from your opponent, always maintain eye contact with your opponent and keep your hands up in order to protect your head and upper body.

3. You and your opponent are now further away from each other in a Closed Position. This "spin back" motion should have taken you out of effective punching range, and put you into an effective kicking range.

4. As soon as the ball of your kicking leg foot touches the ground after completing the "spin back," you should have already begin to execute the kick.

5. Execute the kick.

Did you notice anything wrong or improper in this series of photographs? Take another look. See them now?

Take a look at photograph number two, even though I am still looking at my opponent, see how I have left my back open and exposed to my attacker by not executing both my footwork and turn quick enough. This is not only incorrect, but it is also a very dangerous thing to do. Any technique that you do should be executed so fast that you don't even realize that you have executed it until after it has been completed. **Never turn your back on your opponent.**

Back Spin Out-to-In Axe Kick:
1. You and your opponent are facing each other in an Open Position.

2. Your opponent steps back creating a Closed Position, and increasing the distance between you and him.

3. You "back spin" forward in order to close the distance, which will enable you the opportunity to execute your kick. As the ball of your base leg foot touches the ground after you have executed the "back spin" forward, you explosively complete your turn and...

4. ...begin to execute the kick. Remember, to always keep your eyes on your opponent and your hands up in order to protect your head and upper body.

5. Notice how extremely vulnerable you are in this position. This is why you have got to be so precise in not only the physical aspects or **"How"** to execute the kick correctly, but also the circumstantial aspects or the **"Who, What, Where, When and Why"** for attempting to execute the kick.

6. Execute the kick.

Did you notice anything wrong or improper in this series of photographs? Take another look. See them now?

If you look closely at photograph number three, you can see that I am just a little bit too close to Ron in order to effectively execute an Axe Kick. Therefore, as you can see in photograph number four, I moved my base leg slightly back while simultaneously initiating my kick. Now if you look closely at photographs number five and six, you can see that Ron has either started to duck down in order to avoid being hit by my kick, or he is attempting to tackle me and take me to the ground while my leg is in the air. Even though Ron has attempted to counter my attack, I adjusted to his movement and landed my kick upon his shoulder joint.

Hopping/Sliding Forward In-to-Out Axe Kick:

1. You and your opponent are facing each other in a Closed Position. However, at the moment your opponent is just out of kicking range.

2. Therefore, in order to close the distance with your opponent, you execute a hop/slide forward. As you are moving forward you should begin initiating the kick so that it strikes your opponent at the same time you reach the end of your hop or slide forward.

3. Begin to execute the kick, while adhering to all of the correct principles involved in order to attain the maximum amount of efficiency and effectiveness with your kick.

4. As you hop or slide forward, while bringing your kicking leg up to the "Peak of Arc" position, you can cover anywhere from a few inches to two feet with a correctly executed hop or slide. The exact distance will vary from application to application, but one factor remains. You must be exact in judging the correct distance or your kick will not attain its maximum effectiveness.

5. As you are moving forward you should be executing the kick so that it strikes your opponent at the same time you reach the end of your hop or slide forward.

Did you notice anything wrong or improper in this series of photographs? Take another look. See them now?

If you look at photograph number two, you can see that I clearly executed the hop or slide forward independent of the actual kick. Although this should initially be done in practice until you can effectively combine the two, it should not be done in an actual self-defense situation. If you can not execute a technique perfectly in practice without thinking, you shouldn't try it on the street or in the ring.

Cross-Over In-to-Out Axe Kick:

1. You and your opponent are facing each other in an Open Position. However, at the moment your opponent is just out of kicking range.

2. Therefore, in order to close the distance with your opponent, you execute a "cross-over" motion moving forward. As you are moving forward, you should begin initiating the kick so that it strikes your opponent at the same time you reach the end of your "cross-over" motion.

3. Begin to execute the kick, while adhering to all of the correct principles involved in order to attain the maximum amount of efficiency and effectiveness with your kick.

4. As you "cross-over," bringing your kicking leg up to the "Peak of Arc" position, you can cover anywhere from a few inches to two feet. The exact distance will vary from application to application, but one factor remains. You must be exact in judging the correct distance or your kick will not attain its maximum effectiveness.

229

5. As you are moving forward you should be executing the kick so that it strikes your opponent at the same time you reach the end of your "cross-over."

Did you notice anything wrong or improper in this series of photographs? Take another look. See them now?

In photograph number two, you can clearly see that I have paused for a moment midway through executing the "cross-over" phase of this kick, resulting in my legs being momentarily crossed. This is a very unstable and potentially dangerous position to be in. As soon as the ball of your rear foot touches the ground after "crossing-over" your lead leg, you should have already begun initiating your kick. This is not a mere walking type motion, this is a "faster than you can blink" sprinting type motion. Now if you look closely at photograph number four, you can see that I have both of my arms way to high up in the air, which leaves my body unprotected and throws my balance way off. Especially, since I am balancing on the ball of my base leg foot instead of having it flat on the ground like it should be.

Hopping/Sliding Backward In-to-Out Axe Kick:

1. You and your opponent are facing each other in a Closed Position. While currently at an effective punching range, you are too close to effectively utilize your kicks.

2. Therefore, in order to create a more effective kicking range and in an attempt to deceive your opponent, you begin to execute a hop or slide backwards. Even though you are in effect moving away from your opponent, always maintain eye contact with your opponent and keep your hands up in order to protect your head and upper body.

3. As you and your opponent remain facing each other in a Closed Position, begin to execute the kick. This hop or slide backward should have taken you out of effective punching range, and put you into an effective kicking range.

4. Immediately after hopping or sliding backward, bring your kicking leg up to the "Peak of Arc" position in preparation for executing the kick. You can cover anywhere from a few inches to two feet with a correctly executed hop or slide backward. However, you must be exact in judging the correct distance or your kick will not attain its maximum effectiveness.

5. Execute the kick.

Did you notice anything wrong or improper in this series of photographs? Take another look. See them now?

If you look closely at photographs number three, four, and five, you can clearly see that I have misjudged the distance between Ron and I and had moved too far back. The results of which can clearly be seen in photograph number five, where I have not only missed Ron entirely, but in doing so, gave him the opportunity to grab my kicking foot. Putting me in a very dangerous position. Always create the proper distance before kicking.

Switch In-to-Out Axe Kick:

1. You and your opponent are facing each other in an Open Position.

2. Sensing my opponents impending attack, and wishing to confuse him while repositioning my body, I switch the position of my feet utilizing a scissors type motion. This results in my opponent and I now being in a Closed Position.

3. As soon as the ball of your kicking leg foot touches the ground after completing the "switch," you should have already begin to execute the kick.

4. Always make sure to follow the correct upward "Path of Trajectory" arcing motion up to the "Peak of Arc," which should be as high above your opponent's head as possible, before beginning the downward "Path of Trajectory." Remember to protect yourself at all times and not to telegraph your intentions to your attacker.

5. Execute the kick.

Did you notice anything wrong or improper in this series of photographs? Take another look. See them now?

If you look closely at photograph number two, you can see that I have my body squared directly at Ron, rather than at a 45-degree angle. This is not only incorrect, but it is very dangerous for me as I have exposed a lot more of my body for Ron to attack. After you have become fairly proficient executing this kick, you will find that even though you have switched the position of your feet, your body has remained in the same position. Ideally, if you were able to cover your opponents view of yourself from the waist down, your opponent should never be able to tell that you switched your feet because your upper body shouldn't move. In photograph number five, you can see that even though I have once again struck Ron correctly with my foot, I failed to strike a particular vital or vulnerable point on Ron's head. **I can not stress enough the importance of proper kick placement on your opponent.**

Although it is much better to hit your opponent somewhere on his body rather than missing entirely, it is still nowhere near as effective as hitting the correct vital or vulnerable point.

Awards & Accomplishments

This is a picture of the first world record certificate that I received from the Guinness Book of World Records for performing 10,502 High Kicks in 5 hours and 30 minutes on September 27, 1986 in Butte, Montana USA.

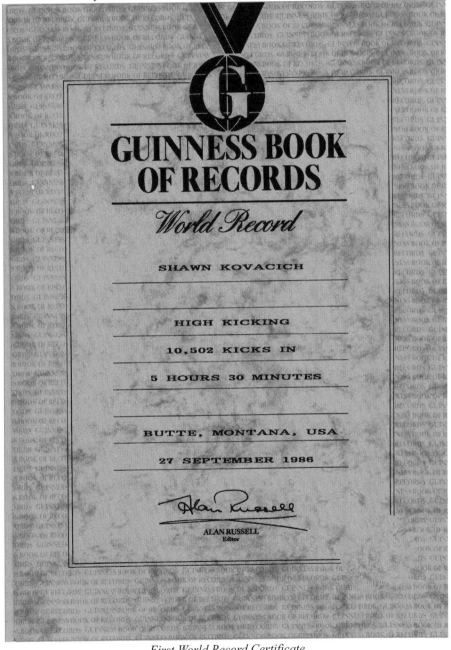

First World Record Certificate

This is a picture of the second world record certificate that I received from the Guinness Book of World Records for performing 11,000 High Kicks in 5 hours 18 minutes and 43 seconds on January 21, 1989 in Anaconda, Montana USA.

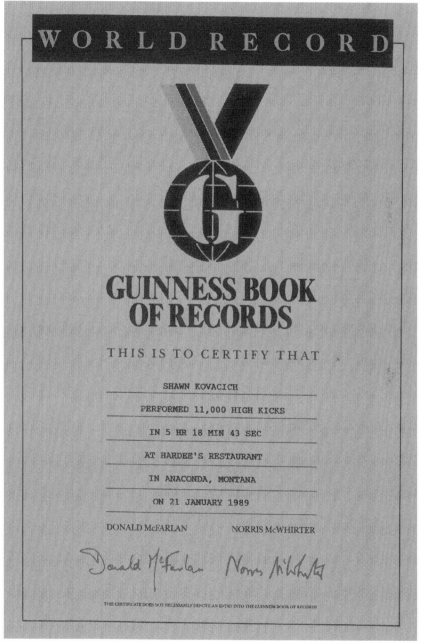

Second World Record Certificate

This is a picture of the actual letter that I received from The Guinness Book of World Records officially recognizing my second world record for performing 11,000 High Kicks in 5 hours 18 minutes and 43 seconds on January 21, 1989 in Anaconda, Montana USA.

GUINNESS BOOK OF RECORDS

Mr S Kovacich   17 March 1989
211B Main
Anaconda
MT 59711
USA

Dear Mr Kovacich

Thank you for sending us the two signed statements as
requested in our letter of 21 February.

We are now in a position to recognise your achievement as a
new record, and unless we receive details of a better claim
before we go to press, your record will be included in the
1990 book. As mentioned in our letter, however, it is a
category which will be dropped after next year's book.

Enclosed is a certificate in recognition of your record -
congratulations.

Yours sincerely

Nicholas Heath-Brown

Nicholas Heath-Brown
Deputy Editor

33 London Road, Enfield, Middlesex EN2 6DJ. England. Tel: 01-367 4567 Telex: 23573 GBR LDN Fax: 01 367 5912
Guinness Publishing Ltd,   Registered Office: 39 Portman Square, London, W1H 9HB.   Registered: London 2079632

The above photograph was taken of me performing an Axe Kick on one of my opponents during a match at the prestigious Sabaki Challenge, which is held annually in Denver, Colorado.

This is another photograph taken of me performing an Axe Kick on one of my opponents during a match at the prestigious U.S. Shidokan Open, which is held annually in Chicago, Illinois.

237

Sneak Preview

Achieving Kicking Excellence;
Volume Four: Crescent Kick

Sneak Preview

Achieving Kicking Excellence; Volume Four: Crescent Kick

Preview of Volume Four: Crescent Kick

The Crescent Kick is one of the ten primary kicks associated mainly with Karate and Tae Kwon Do. This kicked is delivered with a circular, slapping type motion and relies more on speed and momentum for power, rather than actual physical strength. The striking implement utilized in the delivery of this kick is the bottom of the heel or calcaneus, although you can also use the sole and/or ball of the foot. However, the effects of a Crescent Kick are greatly reduced when any other part of the foot other than the bottom of the heel, is utilized. However, under special circumstances, the preferred striking implement will be the sole of your foot rather than the bottom of the heel.

The Crescent Kick is used almost exclusively to an opponent's head and sometimes (although rarely) the lower arm and leg. It is rarely if ever used to strike the body. The primary target points for the Crescent Kick are the temple, nose, jaw, the spine along the back of the neck, the wrist, and forearm up to and including the elbow. Although there are several major factors involved in the correct execution of a Crescent Kick, one of the most important is the proper act of pivoting on the ball of the base leg foot. Many a student has succumbed to unnecessary knee injuries due to a lack of understanding and improper pivoting when executing the Crescent Kick.

The Crescent Kick is not by its very nature a very powerful kick, and due to the increased distance it must travel before striking its target, it is better suited as a set-up technique to be used on your opponent prior to delivering a finishing technique. The Crescent Kick like the Wheel Kick, Axe Kick, Reverse Crescent Kick, Hook Kick, and Hatchet Kick, rely on strong flexibility of the lower back and hips in order to obtain height and correct execution of movement when kicking.

In order to obtain the maximum amount of impact potential in the Crescent Kick, your base leg, kicking leg, hips, and upper body have to be utilized correctly throughout the entire kicking sequence.

Pictorial Overview:Crescent Kick

Fighting Position   Begin Trajectory   Peak of Trajectory

Impact   Follow Through   End of Trajectory

Position #1   Position #2

Recommended Reading

Basic Anatomy of the Back Kick

1. Rasch, Philip J. Ph.D. & Burke, Roger K. Ph.D., Kinesiology and Applied Anatomy, (Lea & Febiger, Philadelphia, Pennsylvania, 1978)

2. Gray, Henry F.R.S., Gray's Anatomy, (Running Press, Philadelphia, Pennsylvania, 1974)

Warm Up and Stretching

1. Anderson, Bob, Stretching, (Shelter Publications, Inc., Bolinas, California, 1980)

Basic Principles of Kicking Movement

1. Fixx, James E., Maximum Sports Performance, (Random House, Inc., New York and Toronto, 1985)

2. Loehr, James E., Ed.D., Mental Toughness Training for Sports, (Stephen Greene Press, Inc., 1986)

3. Mashiro, N., Ph.D., Black Medicine: The Dark Art of Death, (Paladin Press, Boulder, Colorado, 1978)

4. Brancazio, Peter J., Sport Science, (Touchstone/Simon & Schuster, Inc., New York, New York, 1985)

5. Adams, Brian, Deadly Karate Blows: The Medical Implications, (Unique Publications, Burbank, California, 1985)

6. Hibbard, Jack, Karate Breaking Techniques: with Practical Applications, (Charles E. Tuttle Company, Inc., Tokyo, Japan, 1981)

Training and Practice Methods

1. Urquidez, Benny "The Jet", Training and Fighting Skills, (Unique Publications, Inc., Burbank, California, 1981)

2. Derse, Ed, Explosive Power-Plyometrics for Bodybuilders, Martial Artists & other Athletes, (Health for Life, Los Angeles, California, 1993)

241

3. Secrets of Advanced Body Builders, (Health For Life, Los Angeles, California, 1985)

4. Simon, Ilene Caryn, Mind Gains, (Health For Life, Los Angeles, California, 1995)

5. Robinson, Jerry & Carrino, Frank, Max 02 The Complete Guide To Synergistic Aerobic Training, (Health For Life, Los Angeles, California, 1993)

6. The Human Fuel Handbook, (Health For Life, Los Angeles, California, 1988)

Martial Arts & Self-Defense

1. (Lichtenfeld), Sde-Or, Imi & Yanilov, Eyal, Krav Maga: How to Defend Yourself Against Armed Assault, (Dekel Publishing House, Tel Aviv, Israel & Frog Ltd.- North Atlantic Books, Berkeley, California, 2001)

2. Barden, Renardo, Tamashiwara: The Art of Breaking, (Contemporary Books, Inc., Chicago, Illinois, 1985)

3. Tohei, Koichi, Book of Ki: Coordinating Mind and Body in Daily Life, (Japan Publications, Inc., Tokyo, Japan, 1976)

4. Millman, Dan, Way of the Peaceful Warrior, (H.J. Kramer, Inc., Tiburon, California, 1980)

5. Malben, Harris, Muay Thai, (Harris Malben, Helena, Montana, 1976)

6. Fields, Rick, The Code of the Warrior, (HarperCollins, New York, New York, 1991)

7. Little, John, The Warrior Within, (Contemporary Books, Inc., Chicago, Illinois, 1996)

8. Inosanto, Daniel, Absorb What Is Useful, (Know Now Publishing Company, Los Angeles, California, 1982)

INDEX

screw, 62
screwdriver, 62
self-defense, 60
self-discipline, xiii, 105
semimembranosus, 4-12
semitendinosus, 4-12
sequence of movement, 21
Sesame Street, xi
set-up, 156, 212
Shidokan, Team USA, xi
Shidokan, U.S. Open, xi, 237
shoes, 79, 164
shooting, 178
short range, 88
shoulder area, 17
Slide/Hop Backward In-to-Out Axe
Kick, 167-174
Slide/Hop Forward In-to-Out Axe Kick,
159-166
soleus, 4-12
speed, 22-23, 207-208
Spin Back Out-to-In Axe Kick, 65-73
spring, 58, 68
squats, 194-195
squats, hack, 196-197
stability, 18
Step-Back Out-to-In Axe Kick, 92-99
strength, 22
strength training, 155, 194-206
stretching, xv, 13-14, 60, 155
strike through, 63, 81, 104, 126, 179,
212
striking implement, 15-16, 96
surface area, 15-16, 19
surface strike, 16, 63, 212
swimming pool, 208
Switch In-to-Out Axe Kick, 175-182,
183-190
Switch Out-to-In Axe Kick, 84-91

T

Tae Kwon Do, xi, 26, 110, 238
talus, 1-4
tape, 191
target areas, 16-17

telegraphing, 19, 191, 212
temple, 17
tensor fascia latae, 4-12
throwing techniques, 80
tibia, 1-4
tibialis anterior, 4-12
tibialis posterior, 4-12
timing, 23
training methods, 191-210
training partner, 90, 98, 191
trigger, 178
trouble shooting, 170-172
turning, 29

U

upper chest area, 17
USTU, xi

V

variations, 55-108, 139-190
vastus medialis, 4-12
vastus lateralis, 4-12
visualization, 24
vital point, 16-17, 104, 147
vulnerable point, 16-17, 104, 147

W

wall practice, 192-193
warm-up, xv, 13-14
water training, 208
weight, 18
weight lifting belt, 194, 196, 198
weight lifting gloves, 194, 196, 198
Wheel Kick, 238
wood, xiii, 16, 25, 71, 72, 83, 170-173

Notes:

Notes:

Notes:

Notes:

Notes:

Notes:

The only kicking shield ever designed with the serious kicker in mind.

Visit "www.chikara-kan.com" and Order Yours Today!

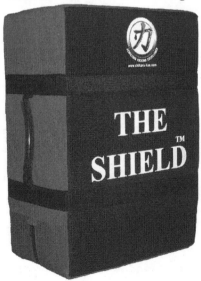
254

Achieving Kicking Excellence™; Applications in Combat™

Volume Thirteen: Axe Kick

Knowing how to correctly execute the Axe Kick is only going to be as effective as your ability to correctly apply the Axe Kick in a self-defense or combat situation. That is why we highly recommend that you also purchase Achieving Kicking Excellence™; Applications in Combat; Volume #13: Axe Kick, in order to learn how to correctly apply this kick in order to maximize its effectiveness.

Please visit our web site at: www.chikara-kan.com and place your order for this and other books in the Achieving Kicking Excellence™ series. And while you're there, we would also like to invite you to submit your review of this, or any of the books in the Achieving Kicking Excellence™ series that you have purchased.

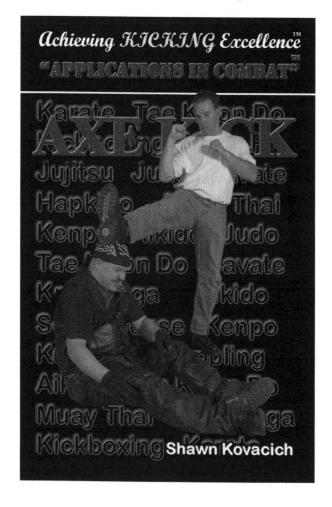

Achieving Kicking Excellence; Defending Against Kicks Volume Twenty-Three: Axe Kick

Knowing how to correctly execute the Axe Kick is only going to be as effective as your ability to correctly defend against the Axe Kick in a self-defense or combat situation. That is why we highly recommend that you also purchase Achieving Kicking Excellence; Defending Against Kicks; Volume #23: Axe Kick, in order to learn how to correctly defend against this kick in order to maximize your effectiveness.

Please visit our web site at: www.chikara-kan.com and place your order for this and other books in the Achieving Kicking Excellence series. And while you're there, we would also like to invite you to submit your review of this, or any of the books in the Achieving Kicking Excellence series that you have purchased.

Achieving KICKING Excellence™

"DEFENDING AGAINST KICKS"

AXE KICK

Shawn Kovacich

256

Made in the USA
San Bernardino, CA
03 June 2018

78323212R00153